WINNER
ENGLISH PEN
AWARD

Carmen Pellegrino is an Italian historian and writer. An eclectic scholar, her research focuses on collective movements of dissidence, racism, social exclusion and the exploitation of migrants (including the essay 'The Hours of my Day', published in the anthology *Qui and Fatigue: Stories, Tales and Reportage from the World of Work*, 2010, winner of the Reportage Napoli Monitor award). Co-author of various collective works, in 2011 she co-edited the volume *Not a Country for Women: Stories of Extraordinary Normality*, which included her essay on Matilde Sorrentino. Among her recent central themes of investigation is the study of uninhabited villages and the ruins of ancient settlements, through which she has laid the foundations for a science of abandonment as a form of recovering awareness of the historical experience of places. In addition to *The Earth is Falling* (*Cade la terra*, 2015), which was shortlisted for the Campiello Prize, Pellegrino is the author of the novels *If I Came Back This Evening Next* (*Se mi tornassi questa sera accanto*, 2017) and *The Happiness of Others* (*La felicità degli altri*, 2021), also shortlisted for the Campiello Prize).

Shaun Whiteside is an award-winning translator from Italian, French, German and Dutch. Originally from Northern Ireland, he has translated many works of fiction and non-fiction, as well as classical and philosophical texts, notably works by Freud and Nietzsche in Penguin Classics. His translation of *To Die in Spring* by Ralf Rothmann won the Sharpe Books HWA Gold Crown for History Writing in 2018 and his translation from the French of *Serotonin* by Michel Houellebecq was long-listed for the International Man Booker Prize in 2021. His reviews have appeared in the *TLS*, *New Statesman*, *Guardian*, *Observer*, *Irish Times* and *Literary Review*.

The Earth is Falling
Carmen Pellegrino

Translated from the Italian
by Shaun Whiteside

To Gerardo and Maria Pellegrino ·
in memoriam

The Earth is Falling

The room will be warm and filled with the smell of fried food. They will all come, in their party clothes and their shoes freshened with a quick brush.

They will come at nine and, one after the other, take their seats around the table. They won't bring presents, they never do, but it doesn't matter: I've got some of my own ready for them, presents that will make their eyes gape, though I'll be looking elsewhere.

As they come in, they won't greet one another, and they won't greet me, but they will gradually make themselves at ease among the freshly caned chairs, around the macramé tablecloth that I use only once a year. They will look around, studying the silent house; then they will yield to the impulse to sniff the air and frown: they haven't come to eat, so why are they here? Then they will sit down and wait. I will bring ricotta ravioli to the table, followed by chestnut dumplings – the chestnuts have been good this year – and last of all dried figs that I have carefully stuffed with walnuts.

For the occasion I have donned my party dress, a fashionable velvet dress ... all right, then, fashionable a hundred years ago. During the first evenings of autumn, in fact, I returned to my lacemaking work and made a white collar that I fixed in place with hidden stitches. Having an abundance of thread, I also made a smaller one – tiny, in fact – from which I hung a little bell, an attachment that makes the most delicate of sounds; it would suit my cat to a T, if I had a cat.

Instead I have a dog, Gideon, who is outside whining ceaselessly. At this time every year, at around dinner time, he starts making tearful eyes and wailing, splitting the silence to which I have grown accustomed. I will have to tell him to stop it, tell him that he can't go on annoying me like this, like a river wind, a wind of premonitions, and besides we both know that the sight of them is all it will take to calm him down.

In the dark days I prepared the room, restoring a little order to the chaos. I polished the old dresser, which roused itself from its torpor with a groan like the sound of glass shattering, and now, to me at least, it has a majestic, imposing appearance. The iron-framed niche on the wall, on the other hand, shrank almost irritably when I slipped my mother's portrait into it: once a year, whether it wants to or not, it's going to have to look after it.

In the middle of the wall overlooking the square there is still an iron grille, even though rust has consumed it from within as worms devour children's bellies. For the moment, I am keeping the curtains open, but later I will need to pull them half-closed, even though my guests will take offence and look at me askance because the window provides their only view of the elm tree. Still, I am forced to do it: if the curtains are drawn, they will not see their faces reflected in the glass; they will not start to tremble.

They never go into the other rooms. And besides, they are closed, the shutters have fallen off, the chairs are covered with little cracks. Every now and again, startled by little bangs, they will glance at one another; then they will give me commiserating looks, and I will do the same, but in this contest of glances I will be the loser. A few hours ago I went to the new town to invite Marcello to dinner, but as usual he didn't seem to hear when I called up from below, asking him to join us, saying we would all be fine together, that we would eat and chat. He greeted me with an offensive gesture from behind his window. I know, though, that

4

he will look at me from behind the smeared glass, then turn up unannounced, saying, 'Here I am again' in that parrot voice of his.

Part One

The House of the Elm Tree

Tornerà, tornerà,
d'un balzo il cuore
desto
avrà parole?
Chiamerà le cose le luci, ivivi?

I morti, i vinti, chi li desterà?

*Will it return, will it return,
with a start will the awakened
heart
have words?
Will it summon things, to lights, to the living?*

The dead, the defeated, who will awaken them?

Alfonso Gatto, *Amore della vita*
(Love of Life)

Estella

I was about eighteen when I started working in the de Paolis house. Where I came from and why, years before, I left my village, needs no recounting here.

It was February and it was snowing the day I came back, an early morning snow that, joining forces with the wind, struck me full in the face in gusts that came and went. Apart from that, silence. I had come back convinced that I could move into the old house where I had lived with my mother until a certain point in time, but I found nothing there. The cottage had succumbed to the soft soil and delivered itself to the earth, adding fresh material to its flourishing anthology of death.

It was cold, but I wanted to see the village again, convince myself that it was not dead, because it could be, I had said to myself as I returned, it could now be dust. I walked along, prey to a fixed idea: was everything I saw really there? Gideon was no help to me; he was shivering with cold and wailing and in a hurry to find shelter. So, to please him, when evening fell – the darkness here has always come quickly – I forced the door of the church, not difficult, rotten as it was. The next day, at break of dawn, they came from Naples to take back my nun's habit, perhaps at the request of the parish priest; they came specifically to rip it from my back, and I was left naked in the churchyard, with the dog doing his best to keep the passers-by from seeing my shame. I remained in that state until I was approached by an old woman dressed in black, who, seeing my sorry state, made no gesture of horror and didn't bring her hands to her eyes, saying 'Lord a-mercy!' as the others had done. She slowly set down the conical basket that she was carrying on her back and with her little wrinkled hands drew out a light, floral-patterned dress of the kind that women wear in the countryside; with a delicate gesture, she brushed away the dust and reached out to give it to me. I immediately put it on as if it were a lambskin blanket, but I didn't have time to thank her, because a moment later the old woman was already far away, swallowed up by the road, with her basket on her back again. I started to walk through the village, leaning from time to time against a little tree which, bruised as I was by the cold, afforded me some modest protection. Very slowly – with Gideon leaping the ditches with the agility of a hunting dog – I dragged myself to the twisted alleyway where the climb to the mountain began, and as I glanced down below everything unwound, everything was clear to me. The village, which had always been on the move, now seemed to have moved even further in its blanket of mud, its inhabitants having retreated northwards to a less tremulous patch of land. There was a strong smell of newly baked bread where there had never been ovens; there were chimneys smoking in alleyways where no one had lived. The tangle of alleyways at the bottom of the hill was in constant retreat – this was also apparent from the discoloured signs of workshops and forges rattling in the wind, and the front doors opening up on to courtyards, these empty too – while people had moved to the streets at the top. I was aware of a touch of regret at having left precisely when the village, as if through some mysterious covenant with death, must have started moving again, battling once more against the stagnant soil, the humps of gravel and red clay. I was discomposed by an unexpected sensation, which I had not yet come to understand. It took a gust of wind to bring me back to where I was, in a mess, with the mountains on all sides, incorruptible guardians of a hole where people went to die, never to be born.

I went back down to the valley via a little passageway, where I observed that life went on as it could, particularly in the square in front of the church to which the old women, drenched from the damp nights, dragged themselves at dawn.

I was cold and hungry – I had eaten perhaps two biscuits in three days – but I managed to summon the strength to introduce myself to the de Paolis family, having read in an advertisement that they were looking for a teacher, to whom they would offer in perpetuity food, lodging and a decent wage.

The house – not far from the centre of the village, facing the elm-tree square – seemed so enchanted to me as to be dreamlike. Two storeys tall, unfenced, it had a small courtyard on which so much snow had fallen that one could barely discern the shapes of a swing and a garden table. I would go on to discover a rocky garden to the rear, with an avenue of pines arranged like sentries, and a little stone fountain, topped when the season was right by amorous turtle doves. I looked at the house in awe for a long time. I couldn't remember there having been such a beautiful thing in the village but concluded that it must have been renovated during the years of my absence.

Struck by a sunless light – a light like the shimmer of the snow – the house quietly dominated the surrounding space, so much so that the village itself, helped by the motions of the landslide, seemed to be shaped around its skeleton. It would soon be morning, but the house seemed to have been awake for hours, as one could tell not least from the carpets that had already been beaten and put out to air on the balconies. I tried to imagine it wrapped in ivy, like the facades of the houses I often saw when wandering aimlessly as a child, before I entered the cloister. I stopped to look at them; houses with balconies that seemed to be supported only by the ivy that held them on either side, the proud ivy that grows wild. I saw women coming out on to the balconies and talking to themselves. But they weren't talking to themselves, they were talking to the ivy, shaking their heads as if in refusal: *no, don't do that.* Then calming down and allowing themselves a smile beneath their deep-ringed eyes – they hadn't slept, those women never did. Once, I impetuously asked one of those baggy-eyed ladies a question. I said, 'Madam, how is the ivy this morning?'

'It is flowering,' she replied, 'or rather it is flowering again. In spite of the frost at night.'

'The frost, you say?'

'The frost, yes, that devours it. But then the dawn comes and renews it all.'

'Madam,' I said, 'you know that I have seen green ivy, so green, on houses that were completely black inside?'

'Don't look inside the houses,' she said, as if she knew what I was referring to, 'Look at them from the outside, look at the ivy. Can't you see that it's like running water?'

Approaching the de Paolis house I saw that the door was wooden with large, delicate-looking glass panels. I turned around and saw the elm tree, standing in lonely iso-lation, its leaves still intact even though it was wintertime. It looked like a monument, a large statue, although it lacked a statue's stillness. It seemed to me, in fact, that it was un-like its reputation, that there was nothing lethargic about it, that it bore no resemblance to those trees that for years moved not at all or barely, broadly speaking. The elm tree, I concluded, was of the clumsy kind, a little tipsy, with roots that seemed to flee the ground with stray ramifications that went where they didn't need to go, the earth having fallen, the stars having fallen. I couldn't have said where that thought came from. I tried to pay it no heed, but the more I thought of it, the more that thought struck me as obvious, almost necessary. The elm tree clearly believed in the benign and illumined force that came from movement, from not keeping everything to oneself. It didn't hold back; it had no interest in conservation. That big tree of sleepless sleep, that clumsy, generous being with its humble scent, believed in the joy that comes from giving oneself, like falling fruit, happy to fall because death comes only to those things that do not give themselves.

Then I heard the sweet music of a radio coming from inside the house, even though the notes were drowned by the hiss of steam from the boiler, which, along with the fireplaces, warmed the dwelling. I decided to knock, and after a moment, as if someone had been keeping an eye on me, the door opened; from behind the door a tall, fat woman appeared, wearing a solemn black dress with a white apron and a white maid's cap, which tilted noticeably to one side.

'Follow me,' she said, with no further formalities, walking ahead of me with a slow, clip-clopping gait.

I would learn that this tall woman was Peppa, the cook and energetic factotum, but above all the most faithful guardian of the walls. The de Paolis family did not ask for references, which was lucky since I had none; they asked no questions, nor were they surprised by my light clothing, unsuited to snowy days. They took me in on that very day because they needed someone to look after their son.

The house's interior was enchanting too: the dining room, in which a clock ticked incessantly, was on the ground floor; next came two drawing rooms, the library and, to the rear, on the other side of the corridor, an airy kitchen with open brick walls and a radio continuously broadcasting gentle music. The bedrooms were on the first floor, while the cellars and the laundry were in the basement, although only Peppa had access to them. I was given a light-drenched room not far from the bedroom belonging to Marcello, the little boy to whom I would be tending. I could not have known it, but the house I was entering was the one in which I would spend the rest of my life, accompanied by fleeting memories and the books that I would peruse over and over again.

According to our agreement, I was to occupy myself solely with the boy's instruction, particularly encouraging him in the study of literature and history, in which I had had the opportunity to immerse myself during my years away. In fact, though, I took him to my heart. He was sixteen years old and extremely thin, his skin taut, his nerves visible. From time to time, talking to Signora de Paolis, I told her that the boy needed robust food to strengthen him – meat stews, potatoes baked in ashes, thick grape syrup, like the one that Peppa made for the adults – but Ada would not hear of the idea of forcing him, adding that a little leanness had never hurt anyone: 'Not even you yourself have any flesh on you,' she said to me, stressing her words by glancing up and down at my bones.

I nonetheless decided to do things in my own way. On the day on which I began my lessons I prepared a cream with egg yolks and sugar, adding a drop of marsala to boost the blood. Then I approached the boy without looking at him and, humming a nursery rhyme to myself, tried to bring a spoonful of the cream to his lips. But at once he flung the cup from my hand and, striking his head with his fists and tearfully crying 'Go away', immediately hurled himself on the floor. I watched him writhing there like one about to suffer grievous torments, while his face, that handsome face of his, contorted into a grimace.

Ada came fearfully running in. Never had she seen him reduced to such a state, she told me, pressing her hands to her face.

'Help me carry him outside,' she said. We struggled to lift him from the floor because Marcello, scrawny though he may have been, was relatively tall. We walked all the way to the square and set him down beneath the elm tree. But just as suddenly he recovered, leaping to his feet like a soldier on parade. He looked at me and smiled, as if he had just played the best trick of the day on me; then he slipped behind the elm tree and lay there on the ground, his body calm, even luminescent.

But I wasn't tricked, not least because the more I looked at him – pale, with a hint of death in his eyes – the more convinced I was that only robust food could save him.

So it was that, some time later, I made my mind up. Early one Monday – the cock had not yet crowed, not least because we didn't have a cock – I took a bowl decorated with ferns painted in verdigris and prepared a zabaglione with six egg yolks, marsala and sugar. When the time came to wake Marcello, I didn't shake his chest as I usually did but tried to sit him up to restore his colour, sleep having left him deathly pale. I laid him on one side – his eyes filled with sleep – and slipped into his mouth a funnel of the kind used in cellars to transfer wine from barrel to bottle. Holding his hands in place firmly beneath my knee, I began to pour the cream down his throat, even hearing a faint glugging sound. Eventually I worried that he might be choking, and was aware of a little shudder, but I didn't stop because I knew the ploys of which he was capable. Once the concoction was gone, I wasn't so foolish as to remove the funnel immediately, because had I done so he would have surely vomited. Instead, I kept it in place even when I was sure it had all gone down, and it was not until he turned purple that I removed the funnel from his mouth, now stained with the yellow cream mixed with the mucus that had somehow flowed from his nose. There was also a stream of blood, but I didn't worry about that. In the effort to recover his breath, with a greed I hadn't expected, Marcello gave no thought to the mixture he had just swallowed, and he didn't vomit. In fact, from the happy regurgitation that rang out across the room I concluded that the method had been the right one. So it was that I began every Monday, at dawn, to pour six fresh egg yolks down his throat, because six would be enough for the whole week. I am sure that it was only in this way that Marcello managed to grow, I would not say strong – because he was never strong – but healthy at the very least.

Marcello

I will go. I will go to dinner. She wants me to go and I will go, if only to see her in that velvet dress that must be a hundred years old.

This morning, as soon as I had awoken, I discovered that her house could no longer be seen from my window. I looked in all directions: it wasn't there. A clear sign that the village is still in motion. This means that I will no longer be able to spy on her. I must tell her that the next house to collapse will be hers, that she will be left underneath it if she doesn't leave. But there is no point, because she won't leave that ditch so skilfully adorned with mist, with all its grass and marshland.

From here, the dead land appears to oscillate like a ship in a storm with all its convex mass, and the prow can no longer be seen from the stern. The foliage that until yesterday hung slackly from the trees has now fallen into the street. The pipistrelles are swiftly reappearing, slipping hither and thither and darting among the ruins. Something always happens with the coming of November: night falls in an instant and nothing can be seen. I know she is in that darkness; I know they are too, darting among the alleyways, whirling together, wandering from party to party, lunch to lunch. I don't understand why they come back.

The room that will house them is not without its charms: the walls retain traces of red paint; there is a big table in the middle, some shelving, a little hearth. In a niche there will be the portrait of a lady in an antique dress from Alento that Estella says is her mother but which might equally be an old newspaper cutting. I am right to believe that Estella identifies it as a portrait of her mother only to prove her Alentese origins, which I refuse to acknowledge. Another of her many lies. She enjoys living a lie. For example, she conceals her vice of smoking, but I know that she toys with a pipe. Every year, on the mantelpiece of the little fireplace, I find tobacco dust, piles of tapped-out ash. 'I have no idea how it got there,' she says, scratching her nose when I point to the tobacco. 'Reality is never unambiguous,' she adds, 'there are dozens and dozens of answers, rebuttals, devastating rejoinders and the like.'

She is joking, she only ever jokes with me, but I will destroy everything that reminds me of her, I will liberate myself from her, that lascivious creature filled only with self-love. She has been like that from the very beginning, since she first entered my life with the fury of a curse. How life is … You might say that my real life lasted for about four years, and the rest I would put down to persistence. I experienced those four years of incinerating beauty when I stopped going to school, at the age of about twelve. One day it was decided that I no longer needed to study with the others, that I was no longer to leave the house. But most importantly, Estella had not yet appeared, which is why I can say with certainty that that was the finest time of my life. But since my happiness was not meant to last, after a sequence of tutors who each arrived and resigned within a month, my parents decided to put their trust in an advertisement:

Governess sought for a lively and intelligent young boy. Food and lodging and a decent wage. For life.

She presented herself with the advertisement in one hand and a string bag in the other.

I would like to describe her as an ugly person, a toad, especially since she was dressed in rags. She wasn't, though. Although she was thin, she wasn't ugly or old: her eyes, staring like an owl's, were blue, a real splash of turquoise, accentuated by the blonde hair that fell to her shoulders. She arrived with a dog, Gideon, a mad, great thing that I never heard barking; it merely whined if it was discontented, and pissed on the gatepost if it was cheerful. When it died, Estella expressed the wish that it be cremated and the remains deposited in a crack in the elm tree; obviously she was indulged, as she would so often be. No one ever asked if I, the future master of the house, wanted her around or not, so dangerously blonde, so pointlessly welcoming. She appeared in my life and my nerves were put sorely to the test; I sulked a little, but to no avail. Besides, her duties were never clear to me: she had been taken on as a teacher, but she soon took an interest in what I ate and in the clothes I wore. It was impossible to understand a thing in that insulting confusion of roles. I knew only that she would always be there with that foxy nose of hers, those eyes that settled on me, making my heart race unexpectedly.

Some mornings she came into my room at dawn without knocking. She would part the curtains and open the window, even if I was sleeping, even if it was stormy. At her touch the shutters squeaked like ducks in flight; she opened and closed them, opened them again and closed them once more so that I would hear the squeak – she wanted me to hear it. In fact she laughed as I turned over in bed. I told her to stop it but she pretended she couldn't hear me. She wanted a fight, that much was clear. When she was done with the shutters, she would come over to me and gaze at me. I would leap out of bed and try to grab her by an arm, but by then she would have turned around and left.

She reappeared when it was time for lessons, which obviously I didn't follow because I cared nothing for any of that wretchedness; it would all have happened even if I hadn't been there. I lived in Alento, amidst ruins, surrounded by hayseeds and a pungent smell of rotting meat.

Towards evening she would come back with a steaming plate, set it down in front of me and stay there, watching me like an owl. Then, from a sleeve, she would take a handkerchief and wipe my nose, in order, she said, to prevent a stray drop falling into the dish, even if there was no drop.

'Swallow your broth, it will do you good,' she said and stared me in the eye.

I took the dish only on the understanding that she would go away; she did, and went and sat beside the hearth. Meanwhile I gulped down the thin brew while spying on her slyly coquettish expression. I spied on her eyes, two glass marbles, and it seemed to me that her eyelids never closed to moisten them; I spied on her stiff mouth, the mouth of someone who has never been kissed; and her hair, yellow as an ear of wheat, which fell to her shoulders, cut into a short tuft over her forehead: she must have had something similar on her unpenetrated quim!

When my father died, I told my mother that to save money we would have to do without Estella, and that she and I would be better off on our own. That's exactly what I said to her, looking her in the eyes so that she would understand that from now on I was the man of the house. She paid me no heed. It was clear that Estella had bewitched her, subjugating poor mother with some sort of spell. And subjugating me too, in one way or another.

At any rate it was the least one could expect from a troubled woman who had entered a convent at a very young age and escaped one night two years later, wearing her nun's habit. They came from Naples to get it back and ripped it off her in front of the church, heedless of the madwoman that she was, leaving her stark naked, her breast covered only by her hair, left long because no one had managed to cut it. Passers-by were left dumbfounded by the spectacle: old men hurried to take pictures of the uncanny sight to tickle their equipment into action when they got home; old women hastily crossed themselves, crying out, 'Lord-a-mercy! She's a mad one!'

Estella

'The dead don't need to be put to bed.' Ada de Paolis said this regularly and with slight concern when anyone came to visit her. Over the years I never saw her withhold her help from anyone, in spite of certain painful consequences – for her son, for example, himself already bereft. In any case, her terrible ministry began only after the death of her husband.

No less than his wife, Giorgio de Paolis was well-liked in the village, so much so that the people of Alento raised their hats when they saw him passing. The poor creatures came to his notary's office, and Giorgio never took their money and, as soon as he saw them rummaging in their pockets for a spare coin, he would show them out with a great wave of his hand. The next day they would come back with baskets full of potatoes, fresh eggs, white flour, and Peppa would take them and thank them as if we were in terrible need of these provisions; they would take off their hats and crumple them in their hands.

His office was towards the rear of the house, reached by a little avenue covered with pine trees that are no longer standing today. On the day of the disaster, they all began hissing simultaneously. It was an April morning and there was no wind. In spite of that, the pine trees trembled. Signora de Paolis must not have noticed, because I didn't see her appear at the window, while I myself had been granted the ability to hear the slightest sound, as dogs are able to do. I went to the door and, even though two or three low clouds followed one another, brushing the treetops, it looked like a quiet spring morning, with the turtle doves affectionately pecking at one another in the nooks of the fountain. I slipped along the avenue and looked at the pine trees: they were two ranks of soldiers that met in the distance; leaning together, they looked at one another and trembled. At the sound, everything, really everything, began to turn to stone, whether it had been killed or merely gone to sleep. First the crests of the bird of paradise plants, which already attracted cries of astonishment, were listless filaments, falling to one side or another. The geraniums, meanwhile, looked exhausted in the crêpe-lined pots, like open sores in the sun. A little further away, swarms of insects fled to expire in the moss, while beneath my feet suddenly fallen young leaves shrank and groaned. I walked on and, unintentionally, crushed the buttercups that had thrown themselves to the ground. I looked at the tongues of the maple, which seemed mangled by an excess of light; I looked at the branches of the cherry tree, suffering from an excess of shade. The light separated itself from things and broke down into its component parts according to no rule in particular. The stone fountain, in the middle of the path, was out of water and seemed about to crumble to dust. Here and there one could spot deformed rocks tumbling into the ditches or nestling in the cracks of the flowerbeds, revealing deserted, abandoned anthills. I saw a worm with a severed abdomen and heard a strange hissing sound as it reassembled itself and continued slowly on its way. I looked up and a fly came and settled on the ridge of my nose: its face looked diseased, and its eyes were pleading; I shooed it away but only sent it sliding down to the tip, where it promptly fell asleep. I reached the aviary at the end of the avenue and was surprised to see our goldfinches, normally slow and slightly mad, beating against the bars as if an earthquake were coming. I sat down on a bench and collapsed as well, falling asleep without the slightest resistance.

It was only when the rustling song of the pines came to an end – I have no idea how long it took – that everything returned to the way it had been before: I woke with a start, and with me the fly, which flew away embarrassed. Then the fountain started gushing water once again, the rocks left the ditches one by one and even the insects recomposed themselves, while all around the leaves and flowers began to breathe again with relief.

That day, the parish priest sent for Giorgio de Paolis as a matter of urgency. The church was in danger of collapsing from the damage caused by the landslide, and the side facing the hill, which had remained intact for many years, was cracked. Since no maintenance work had been done since the collapse of the choir roof, the time had come to act. Besides, de Paolis had always been generous to the church – he had, for example, donated some pews, besides the two reserved for his family, which were sited in positions crucial for holy protection against evil influence. After lunch and a very short nap that must have seemed a breath's duration, Giorgio set off for the church. It was just past three when the sky darkened and released hailstones so fat that within moments the streets, the houses, the square, were covered in icy white. The storm didn't last long, but it was the prelude to a ballet of lightning flashes of a kind seldom seen. One bolt struck the church just as de Paolis was climbing the steps. He fell in the worst way imaginable, and there was nothing to be done: he died in an instant, a mere black puppet.

Marcello

I was twelve when I was taken out of school. They said that I would have to be taught at home, because I refused to pay attention in class or even to stay at my desk. Furthermore, the fear of illness kept me from the others. A fear that was far from unfounded. I knew, for example, that my little schoolmates didn't wash their hands when they went to the toilet. I had seen them with my own eyes, hurrying to do up their flies after doing their business and coming out, ignoring the most basic norms of hygiene. Then, when they showed obvious signs of illness, I deployed a kind of mask that I kept hidden in my satchel: no sooner had they started sneezing or coughing than I put it over my nose and mouth.

It was true that I didn't pay attention in class, that I didn't sit at my desk like a great lump hanging on the words of people like Elisa Serri, a hairy old maid with the most goatish of beards on her chin.

'De Paolis!' she cried. 'We need to tie you to your desk, that's what we need to do.'

'Miss!' I replied. 'We need to shave that beard of yours, that's what we need to do.'

My mother reacted badly to my removal from school and informed the headmaster that from now on they would have to do without our donations. As for myself, I would go on studying at home with the best available tutors while the rest of them went on wriggling about within those walls. I was happy no longer to have to set foot in that penitentiary, crammed with yokels who gave off the smell of the stable from early morning, even though their confinement to the desks below the windows did something to attenuate the stench. And besides, it was well known that they brought lice into the school; they had them growing everywhere, even on their eyelids.

One was the most gangling of the lot. His name was Bonaventura Paudice, and he had black under his nails as if he'd been raking soil with his hands. In the morning he would break off a bit of bread with suet – the entirety of his breakfast – and try to give it to me. He thought I was his friend because I had once given him a figurine of which I had two: his eyes gleamed like Christmas balls on the tree. Since then, he had followed me around like a dog. He wasn't annoying, I must admit, but he was dirty, and even his teeth were something you wouldn't have wanted to look at: they were all over the place. He lived in the countryside down below the village, in a cottage without a toilet that was also a store for provisions and a stable for animals. He was said to sleep on a mattress stuffed with corn husks.

For his part, Paudice ignored such stories, and it was even believed that he fed these stories himself. However, he was the only member of his family ever to have set foot in a school. He turned up to class exactly on time every day. After school he looked after his father's sheep or sheared them to sell on the wool. As to his mother, it was said that she knew how to make potions out of weeds, or poultices and the like. It was rumoured that she could heal wounds with her piss, the same that she used to water the parsley that she would sell to the few who ventured as far as her house to purchase it in large quantities.

The three of them only came up to the village on days of obligation, washed but with their faces the colour of soil, their hands the colour of leather. Once Mass was over they returned to the fields; the village was no place for them. There they found the sheep and the puddles waiting for them, and the hovel they lived in, at least until the day it collapsed. That night they turned pale with terror.

Marcello had no friends to visit, and no one ever came to ask to meet him. No one, no one at all had ganged together with him as young boys tend to do. Marcello hated the villagers, but the ease with which he displayed his fundamental hatreds was based on one simple fact: he was only the last link in a chain of hatreds that came down the generations.

For a long time I pondered how to escape from the whirlpools that lure us to drown ourselves, but I never managed to find an answer. I concluded that we all partake in such inherited passions, which become more stubborn the more constant our contact with others. Still, I had never managed to get beyond those beginnings.

Marcello belonged to a centuries-old tradition of resentments that had acted upon him most successfully, stripping him of any chance to know the things of the world with greater intimacy; concealing from him the impulse – which I too recognised in him – to approach others without the armour of his privilege. Swathed in a tangle of hostilities that burned instinctively, Marcello acted with a tender cruelty. I had confirmation of this one afternoon, when he staged an unexpected piece of theatre.

I was in the square, staring at the newborn twigs of a bunch of mistletoe, whose tentacles gripped the elm tree with alien tenderness, so much so that it was hard to tell where one began and the other ended. The elm tree had fought a personal war against the parasite's intrusion and had irritatedly tried to lift its branches higher, the effort making it look like the inverted skeleton of an umbrella, albeit one covered with leaves. But since the battle could not be waged indefinitely, the tree had eventually returned its branches to their original position. I was busy observing it, convinced that some meaning must lurk in those intrusions, when I remembered I had left the front door of the house ajar. Fearing that a gust of wind might shatter the glass, I ran home, even though to tell the truth there wasn't really any wind to speak of. When I reached the doorstep, I went to grip the handle – but the two panels opened together, then crashed noisily shut again, although without shattering. Surprised, I looked inside, and no sooner had I crossed the threshold than I saw a shadow slipping along the corridor. I immediately thought of some forest beast, a wolf or a scrawny boar of the kind that are seen often in these parts, but then it appeared to me as if the shadow was lengthening and turning into a human one. I saw it only vaguely at first; then more clearly, as it approached the wall. When I reached the corner where the carpet runner led to the kitchen, the shadow continued on, turning for barely an instant to check that I was following. When it did so I could see its face, curved, and covered with a floral-patterned oilcloth of the kind used in the kitchen. I approached, and, as it raised its head towards me, I thought I could see a brief gleam through the eyeholes, but otherwise it was like peering through frosted glass. I resolutely clutched at the hem of the oilcloth and, emitting a strange serpentine hiss, there before me was Marcello, calm and smiling.

'What on earth are you doing?' I asked him, holding him back by his arm, even though there was no need because he was perfectly serene.

'Don't ask any questions, just follow me,' he replied, heading for the stairs that led to the bedroom.

I decided to follow. He walked slowly, hugging the wall.

He turned around twice, gesturing to me to say nothing, his index finger pressed to his lips.

We entered his room, and I immediately noticed the outline of a man on a chair: he had his back to us and had a straw hat pressed down over his head, with a purple ribbon, like the hat that Ada de Paolis wore on summer days. I saw that the man was tied up, bound with a rope to the back of the chair.

'Who is this?' I asked, turning towards the man, while from the corner of my eye I looked at Marcello, who was pacing up and down on the mosaic of the floor, stretching as if in preparation from some great effort. 'Who is this?' I repeated.

'He won't reply, he's a scoundrel. If you approach him you'll smell just how much he stinks,' and Marcello rubbed his knees with an expression of satisfaction.

'Who is this man?'

'He's a scoundrel, I told you.'

'And why is he here?'

'I've taken him prisoner, can't you see? I just needed a rope,' he said, just like that, and then he broke into that little peal of laughter he had, always ready, high-pitched and shrill.

'What are you thinking of?' I tried to shout, but my voice barely emerged.

'He was on my property, around the back, staring at the house. I saw him narrowing his eyes to focus on the windows and the doors, stock still in the avenue. His legs – you should have seen his legs: they were crossed in an X, like when you're about to piss yourself. I could tell straight away that he was a thief.'

It was then that I approached the man. I walked around

him, but his head was lowered; I lifted his chin with a finger to see his face and nearly had a stroke. There, wrapped up like a parcel, was good old Giacinto, the town crier who, day after day, wandered the streets and alleys of the village to publicise actions taken by the authorities or announce developments in the progress of the landslide. He was lame and blind, but not entirely: he could see something, shadows at least, which kept him from wandering down paths where he wasn't supposed to go.

When I freed him from the rope, I saw that he had a ball of cloth stuffed into his mouth to keep him from shouting. Since his neck was stiff and he was unable to lift his head, I left him alone for a moment. I knew then that Marcello had really thought of everything, and I could see his eyes gleaming. He had forced a man into a kind of prison, and I couldn't believe it. For the first time since I had moved into that house, I felt the urge to slap him in the face, to strike that sniggering mouth of his. I was so upset that I couldn't move. I of all people, who protected him as best I could against the world outside, which didn't exist for him; I of all people, who was little more than a playmate, even though it had been my duty to care for him with a maternal instinct that I lacked; at that moment I could have thrashed him. However, stretching my patience to the limit, I merely gave him a sidelong look. Then I spoke.

'I will tell your parents. You will have the punishment you deserve. I'm not going to cover for you this time.' And, gripping him by an arm, I manoeuvred him out of the room. He merely smiled at the threat of punishment, then freed himself from my grip and hugged me before running away.

As if in a daze, Giacinto slowly rose from the chair to which he had been bound for who knows how long, and

33

explained to me that today he had struggled to find his usual route and that, in a failed attempt to regain his bearings, he had ended up at the back of the house.

'What happened next?' I asked him, guessing the darkness of what would follow.

'A boy's voice from a window says, "Who are you?" I answer, "I'm Giacinto the bellman." Then the voice says: "Liar, you don't have the trumpet or the hat of a town crier." I tell him: "I don't need the trumpet because I can shout louder than any brass instrument, but I'll have the hat soon: they're sending me one from the factory." And then the voice says: "Wait for me there."'

'I imagine he then came down and got you,' I said.

'Not exactly. Once he was down there, without a word he threw a rope around me, and then we stayed like that for a few minutes – I didn't move, I was confused. It was only when I tried to free myself from the noose around my neck that the boy came over. "It's worse if you struggle," he said, and dragged me away, shouting: "The man in black fell in a trap. The man in black fell in a trap."'

'Were you scared?'

'By the Holy City, miss, I was shitting myself!'

Marcello

The yokels never missed an opportunity to show their true calling: to grab as much as possible from their time with the gentlefolk and sell themselves for a handful of grain, trusting that God himself would supply the rest: 'This year I sowed five *tomoli* of grain, I hope the Lord Almighty will give me twenty in return.' They were unequalled in their reliance on miracles to combat their own inertia.

One of the places the yokels came to was my house. Every time they came, asking to speak to my mother; every time they brought their faces within those walls, I cursed Estella for throwing open the doors to them, summoning them like a plague of rats. What I'm trying to say is that for some people, taking their noses out of their bogland and sticking them into our house was pretty much the same as stepping into paradise.

More than anything, I was worried about the effect that all this coming and going would have on my mother. Her face went into a spasm as soon as Estella announced a new visit; she nodded furiously, but it was clear that she was frightened. Then she touched her forehead and slipped away to join the new throng.

They all kept themselves to the little drawing room, which was furnished with a dark green chaise longue and a truly hideous oval painting of a dishevelled-looking man holding a bunch of poppies.

My mother closed the door from inside, so they were locked in for hours. I tried to eavesdrop, especially the first few times, but the noise of the chairs moving around drowned out the words.

The fact that she shut herself in a room with men with

calloused hands and who knows what else gave me the right to think evil thoughts, and I won't say that I didn't, particularly at the beginning. Let's say that at the beginning I spied on them. But however much I spied on them, I never saw bodies writhing or clothes being flung in the air. All I saw was this: my mother sitting on the *feuille-morte*-coloured chaise longue and a man (later, women would turn up as well) standing in front of the hearth with his back to the fire.

One afternoon, one of the last people still living in the old town turned up, an old, half-drunk sluggard. He was enormous and moved by lifting his legs with his hands. Without a word he walked towards my mother, looking around as if he were in a strange world far from his own. My mother asked him if he needed anything, and the sluggard made a strange sound in his gullet that might have meant yes, why not. A moment later he slumped on a chair, took a bottle of grappa from his pocket and cleared his throat by taking a swig.

'I have spent so much time sitting down and in silence,' he said after a pause during which we gaped in silence, 'that I can't walk, I don't even know how to speak.'

'Don't worry, Cola, tell me what I can do for you.' My mother had recognised that enormous lump of ethylated flesh as old Cola Forti, the anarchist who some years previously had had a number of difficulties related to certain aspects of his fanatical enthusiasms.

'My dear madam,' he began, dabbing his forehead with a handkerchief to absorb the broad swathes of sweat, 'a man once said, "What we want for everyone is bread, freedom, love and science." That was a long time ago. Should you ever have the opportunity, please do inform him that I believed it, at a certain point in my life I believed it. Then, when I worked out that what I had believed with a lunatic's obstinacy was an illusion, I sat down on the bench under the pergola and never moved again. Should you wish to pay me a visit, that's where you will find me. Now that it's all over, I would appreciate a word of consolation on your part.'

I gave my mother a puzzled look: this man had allowed his life to be defined by four nouns, and now he spent all his time sitting under a pergola! I was clearly in the presence of an idiot.

My mother didn't even look at me, she was too busy nodding at the sluggard. Whatever I might have imagined, those two were imagining more, behind my back.

After another swig of grappa, the old man extended his hand to my mother in a gesture of farewell, without a trace of reverence. Then he made for the door, followed by Estella, who immediately offered him her arm so that he could stay upright, meanwhile unsheathing a silvery smile with a flash of the eye, typical of the chilly coquette that she was. She had never smiled at me in that way.

That was what made me decide to make her pay, that very evening, in the only way I could think of, not least because I had very limited means at my disposal. It was just after ten when I slipped from my room; my mother had withdrawn for the night and Estella was about to do the same.

As soon as I heard the click of the lock (clearly it was Estella locking it from inside), I went downstairs and, leaning against the wall of the corridor, began to make myself sick. A moment later, I pissed on it and mushed the whole thing up with my foot. A steaming, yellowish pool appeared before me, with little strips of food standing out in the brew like human figures in Flemish paintings.

Then I took a lump under my foot and dragged it down the corridor to the kitchen; then I turned back and, again using my foot, drew circles of muck on the skirting board, bigger and bigger, finishing with a huge circle on the front door, which was made of the very finest glass. When I was satisfied, I sat down on the floor to contemplate my accomplishment, but since such a refined piece of work deserved an audience, I shouted: 'Estella, Estella, my dear, come and see what I have done.' She came running and brought her hands to her face as soon as she saw the lovely mess.

'Now smile at me too,' I said to her, enjoying the sight of her down on her knees, cleaning away. It was without a doubt one of the finest moments of my life.

Estella

It was after the death of her husband that Ada de Paolis began locking herself away in the drawing room with the picture of the poppies, at first every now and again, then more and more often. As soon as I realised what was happening within those walls, I did everything I could think of to stop her, but she refused to listen to me. I came to discover that she could not do otherwise: without her husband she was like a river without banks, a heart training itself to die, playing dead among the living and living among the dead. Today I wonder if she hadn't made the right choice.

It's madness to imagine that you need only cling to what remains. In fact the opposite is true. We sit near the dead who become so dear to us, we listen to the words whose meaning dwells within us, and all we have to do is acknowledge the fact. Sometimes the dead repay us, when they come home in the strangest forms. Besides, they never go away completely, just as among the living no one is ever entirely here. Among the dead we can stop covering up our grief with the sound of bells in a stubborn attempt to chase it away. Grief goes about its journey, which is often hard to grasp. Sometimes it becomes inert, like a scar. At other times it wedges itself like a thorn beneath a fingernail and stays there. At any rate it is something we all share. That was why Ada de Paolis saw her own grief in the grief of others, in the same sincere and unquestionable way, and felt a part of it. She placed her trust in the acceptance of signs, of coincidences that pointed to the fragility of the boundaries between us and them. She said that we don't need cemeteries to meet them, and she convinced herself of this by observing how the sun, on certain days, rose unexpectedly from its depths; on those days she sat and watched the water flowing or the swaying of trees.

I was still struggling to grasp what was going on: I couldn't believe that I had to encounter this nameless thing, the very thought of which made me tremble from head to toe, so prematurely and so often. Then, when I saw so many making themselves at home within our walls, participants in a conspiracy that had nothing dark about it, I understood that the insurmountable was but a threshold that held us, as in the bubble of a dream. This house, partially spared by the landslide, was fashioned with the precise intention of becoming their final dwelling place. That's why they come back. That's why it's my home.

It started when the rotting body of Giorgio de Paolis was brought to the house. Ada didn't immediately approach the puppet that was now her husband – an imposing man who could have been a film star, with his elegant grey hair, sharp, straight nose and slow, very slow way of speaking, as if reading something from a sheet of paper. Now he was entirely hard and black, a tree trunk. The men who had hoisted him from the church square and carried him home in their arms deposited him in the hall before removing their hats and crossing themselves several times.

Ada looked at him.

'What sort of a joke is this?' she said, bringing to her face first one hand, then another.

'Oh, my Giorgio!' she said over and over again. 'Oh Giorgio, I wish you could wash yourself, because it's nearly dinner time and we don't sit down at the table with dirty hands.'

For a moment she took her eyes off that vision which I didn't know whether to attribute to my imagination or rather to fate's relentless torment of our family, and I saw that Peppa had appeared in the corridor. Her features were barely distinguishable, immersed as they were in shadow, but I saw that she was holding an unfolded sheet. I gestured to her to come forward and cover the body, which she did.

'I don't recognise him under the shroud for the dead,' Ada said, turning to me a few moments later, and in her voice there was a little of the mournful singsong that precedes weeping, the moment before the floodgates open.

'Carry him over there, into the room with the poppies. Peppa will show you the way,' she said, before turning to the men who had brought the body home.

Then again to me: 'I don't know what will happen next, but I know that Giorgio will speak tonight, and I will hold him close to me, my breast is still warm.'

After saying this, she locked herself away in the little drawing room and only reappeared two days later, when she finally agreed to the funeral. In any case, her face looked relaxed to me: whatever grief she might have suffered she appeared to have forgotten.

'The mist rose early this morning,' she said to me as we walked along the avenue in procession behind the coffin, carried on the shoulders of six men. 'It's a lovely day for a funeral.'

Of the countless faces that wandered through those rooms in search of the goodness that it emanated I have only a confused memory: some appeared only once, others stood out with the constancy of their visits, the scruple with which they introduced themselves. Among the latter was a man who had already found his sense of destiny in the very thin line dividing the two worlds. His name was Maccabeo.

I would like to remember him because, for as long as he could, he came to our house bringing with him an aura of joy, unusual in visits of this kind. He was a gentleman, quite old, about ninety, with a thick white beard that the wind ruffled like the feathers of a chicken, revealing the flesh beneath. On the journey from his house to ours some people saw him kneel and remain calmly there for a certain period of time, immersed in prayer. Sometimes I too found him hunched in a corner of the house, motionless; after a while he would get back on his feet and cheerfully rejoin everyone else. He carried with him a bag full of books, and when Marcello took it from him as a joke, throwing the books in the air, we discovered that they were accounting books. The good man did not lose his temper but picked up what was left of them and smiled at us without a hint of reproach. Not even when Marcello started insisting that he take his shoes off at the front door – at times when he was seized with the fear of disease – did this good fellow react badly; it was always better to go with it, he said. Nonetheless, he soon developed the habit of carrying with him, along with the books, a pair of slippers to avoid going barefoot.

One day, as I waited for Ada to return from a visit, Marcello turned quizzically to Maccabeo. 'Have you seen the stone commemorating my father outside the church?' he asked, looking at his fingers.

'It is beautiful,' the man replied.

'The hell it is! A serious error has been committed in the transcription of his surname: De Paolis has been carved a capital D, erasing my father's noble origins.'

'No great harm is done, young man. In the beyond, among the dead, no one will pay it any heed,' Maccabeo said, and rested his hands in his lap before returning his gaze to the window, patiently awaiting Ada's arrival.

Marcello burst out laughing, a tinny peal as usual, before withdrawing. The following day he insisted on preparing a cup of tea for Maccabeo. No one intervened to dissuade him. I only discovered that evening that not only had he urinated in the teapot, he had also daubed the edges of the cup with a paste of worms diluted with hot water. It was he himself who told me, with a kind of animal triumph.

Marcello

My annoyance at the yokels who besieged my house lasted
for as long we remained in the old village, since my mother
threw the doors open to them, and I could never understand why. They came to our house whenever they liked,
they came to drink from the cups that Estella promptly
filled with coffee or cocoa, and they were overwhelmed by
the idea of being able to sip a liquid that was not their usual
daily broth. As they drank, they emitted sucking noises
that would have made cows blush, and talked only of other
poverty-stricken wretches afflicted with revolting illnesses,
or of feuds and betrayals, so that a large part of the village
met up in our house.

The apogee was reached when my mother, at the
urging of the Sisters of Charity, agreed to 'give the poor
of the village some hours of relief and joy on the occasion
of the impending Christmas festivities', and that relief
was to be provided at our house.

The idea was received with enthusiasm by the
ludicrous elite of Alento. They said that what was required
was a fine and humanitarian celebration, when what
they really needed was an opportunity to cleanse their
consciences in advance of Christmas. At our expense.

Estella's face became coloured by a dangerous
contentment and, to get everything ready in time, she set
about the task like a dog chasing a hare. It was clear that
she needed only to have her peers around her to reach a
state of fervour; it was also apparent from the gleam in her
eyes, which were usually a mummified blue.

Two days later, a gigantic Christmas tree was erected
in the drawing room, with an explosion of bags of candied

fruit and chocolate on its branches.

On the evening of 23 December, the children of the local bumpkins turned up at our door and suddenly they were scattering along our corridors, looking around open-mouthed. One, seeing a brass banister, exclaimed 'It's gold!' and I nodded furiously because there was no point explaining the difference.

Once they had calmed down, I set about observing them in greater detail. They looked entirely out of place, and their party clothes made them look as if they came from another era.

The boys had severe side partings in their hair; among the girls, one, in a brimless hat, stood out. Her name was Lucia Parisi, and she had been a classmate of mine for several years. Modestly dressed, even clean, she lived in the countryside around Terzo di Mezzo, but she wasn't stupid, and the teachers didn't see her as having a passive disposition, unlike the others. In spite of this, she stopped going to school early, even before I did. When the time came for her to take off her hat, she tried everything she could think of to remove it and kept it on her head for the whole evening like a bonnet, which gave her a particularly wild appearance. Peeping out from beneath it, her eyes were wide with amazement at finding herself in an enchanted place, and they darted here and there. Turning slowly around, she stared now at the porcelain statues, now at the stuccos on the walls; she stared at the silverware and the crystal glasses, even at the books and paintings. She could not break away from those visions. It was as if she had begun a journey of her own, and her eyes were discovering a world that had until then been denied to her. At one point she tripped over her feet and stumbled; embarrassed, she remained on the floor for a few minutes, until Estella ran over to give her a piece of chocolate. She recovered immediately upon biting into it.

On that particular evening she had been accompanied by her father, one Consiglio Parisi, who waited for her on the stairs. Eventually, my mother joined him. I saw them talking with such familiarity that I could no longer help myself and went to eavesdrop, but I was disappointed: the man was talking about a daughter by the name of Mariuccia, who had died, and my mother was comforting him. I waved my hand to ward off bad luck and moved away. Later I would see him on other occasions at our house, in search of my mother, who allowed him a degree of intimacy that I found troubling. And, to make things worse, she obliged me to do the same.

On this particular evening the other guests weren't doing much but looking around, clustering by the tree, covered as it was with goodies, and clambering over each other when my mother dished out handfuls of sweets. If until then they had seemed dazed, in an instant they became alert, wiping their watery eyes on their sleeves and hurrying to receive them. At one point I saw that one of them was standing in a little puddle of urine; I looked at my mother in disbelief, but she was looking elsewhere. When the time came to say goodbye, they gathered in the corridor; seen from the top of the stairs they formed a ragged procession, leaving for the new world.

Outside those beautiful, humanitarian occasions, the yokels were left to freeze. The warmth bestowed upon them, the generosity afforded them by the wealthy on the occasion of these festivities, was merely a show conditioned by huge and multiple interests. The bumpkins came up to the village only on holy days; the rest of the time they lived in the countryside below. Shepherds, horse dealers, cowherds and others; the school held their children in place at desks beneath the windows, allowing their stench to escape through the cracks. It was the same in church: they stayed at the very back, exhausted but erect, hearing words about sacred mountains but knowing only their own.

My father had given the parish two pairs of pews: one belonged to us by right, and in fact it was reserved for us, as was apparent from the little brass sign with our surname engraved on it – this was the pair near the altar, on the left, just below the statue of the Madonna of the Landslide, without question the best position in the church. The other pair bore no sign, which meant it was available to anyone. The fact is that the yokels never sat on those pews, not even when, after a piece of the church roof collapsed, the gentry no longer obliged them to keep to their own rows, given that strong arms were needed for the building's reconstruction.

My father's pews were joined by others donated by other wealthy families, all very respectable and religious, and in constant conflict with one another about where exactly the pews were to be placed. The parish priest suggested a half-yearly rotation, from which the yokels were obviously excluded, even though they had no objections. After all, they knew too: once Mass was over they had to return to the fields, because community was something that other people had. They were left with the sheep, to be shorn three times a year, and the stinking puddles that no one drained, and the weeds, the poison darnel, the clover and all the medicinal herbs they could want. Sooner or later, someone would leave the village and go into the marshes in search of plants for concoctions, poultices, potions and cures. In such cases, the community came together. It gave the yokels a moment's laughter.

Estella

Many Alentesi passed through that house: the village came inside and gradually faded away, leaving its shadow on the walls, a shadow that lies there still, a whole legacy that remains of those years. I am not left with much, I know. Besides, how could I be so presumptuous as to hold on to more than the grace of a shadow that passed across the walls, if outside the wind has broken the shutters and inside the plaster is flaking? In my memory I carry the gestures, the caresses of moments recalled, while ahead of me is nothing but the house's way of being self-contained, turning in circles like a dying animal in search of rest. I will not believe pointlessly in perpetuity; I am well aware that the house will not be there forever, I can see the cracks, the splits in its structure. When I approach the walls I stroke their surface, I touch it like wounded skin. So, I think, while it resists – if this big house holds out, if it holds out even in this condition, if it can really do that – then I can hold out too, on good days and bad, one wound after the other, in this temporary dwelling, lingering on in this place a little longer, just a little longer.

Then there are the others; the house awaits them, even though it looks as if it has had the worst of bad nights, even though so much of it is broken. They plainly care: I see them looking around, looking at the beams; still, possessed as they are by waiting, they always approach the house as if approaching a bride. I receive them in the room that looks out on to the elm tree – the tree in thrall to the night that frees us from reality's affliction – and together, in daylight, we believe that we are levelling destinies.

Once, towards the end of a rainy March, even the

parish priest begged us for hospitality when part of the rectory collapsed after a sudden shift in the landslide, and we had no option but to take him in.

His hair pomaded, Don Basilio appeared in the afternoon with a great rustle of vestments, and after talking at length to Signora de Paolis about the landslide and his rheumatism he sat down at the table, announcing with a rumble of his stomach the hunger that consumed him. His nostrils were perpetually dilated and his eyes avid for the slightest motion of crockery, and he had a pot belly that could have afforded more shelter to numerous animal species than many a tree. Once he had chosen the position most comfortable to his abdomen – the abdomen so confused with his bladder that the peasant folk had awarded him the nickname of 'pee bucket' – he summoned Peppa with a wave of his arm, ordering her to bring him a hot broth, which would without a doubt warm his bones. The rain had been pouring in torrents for days, as it sometimes does in these parts. The priest didn't seem worried: all that he could hear was the call of his belly, and so after the broth, which seemed barely to have calmed his appetite, he invited us to sit down so that the real dinner could begin. Ada was visibly irritated but didn't express her thoughts aloud.

There were only three of us at table because Marcello preferred to remain in his room and was usually not greatly disposed to intrusions of this kind.

'What terrible slavery it is to have a working digestive system,' the priest began as soon as he had the roast (surrounded by potatoes and raisins) in front of him. 'Yes, because at the same moment the entire mechanism is completed,' he added, biting into the first substantial mouthful.

'To what mechanism are you referring?' Ada asked; like

me, she had not failed to notice a sluicing noise emanating from the priest's gullet.

'The ingestion and expulsion of food, my dear madam. Whatever some may say, these things are determined here and now, at the table, even though the purgation will take place subsequently, on a seat of a different kind. Our stomach puts us immediately and forever at the mercy of our innards, and the whole process occurs unequivocally at the table.'

'Do you not find this subject-matter inappropriate at a laid table?' she asked, her proud little mouth quivering with alarm.

'Repugnant though it may be, my dear Ada, this is the inescapable cycle of every living creature. There is nothing else.'

'It is curious that you of all people should say this,' she said, giving him a contemptuous glare.

'Poppycock!' he exclaimed. 'I shall quote, Psalm 138, *For you created my inmost being*, etcetera, etcetera. *I praise you because you made me*, etcetera, etcetera, *marvellous are your works, I know that very well...*'. His mouth was full of meat as he spoke and, without setting down his fork, he gulped one after the other the potatoes that remained on his plate.

It was then that Ada, referring to an indisposition that she almost certainly didn't have, got up and left the room; as she took her leave, I watched her from the corner of my eye and caught a flash of disdain in hers, a flash to which the priest appeared oblivious. I remained alone with him at the table; he remained cheerful throughout, although the vapours that escaped his control from time to time gave me the sense of a harmful stagnation at work in that bladdery body.

After dinner we sat down in the drawing room, not far from the window that looked out on the elm-tree square. We decided to take some tea. At that time of the evening, two or three moonbeams struck the tip of the tree so that the shaggy mass resembled a huge old man with a white beard.

'This, my dear Estella, is the right night for ideas,' the priest said to me at some point, as if talking to himself, as he sank into the armchair that had once been Signor Giorgio's.

'For ideas?' I asked him, staring at his fingers, which, twirling a half-cigar, seemed to mime a swift count of banknotes.

'Yes, my dear. It is four months until the feast of the Madonna of the Landslide and I must restore the statue's dress.'

'What happened?' I asked, betraying a certain apprehension, because the Feast of the Landslide was one close to everyone's heart, so much so that for the whole month of July the village was in a state of ferment, the streets filled with arches of light, coloured panels and standards reproducing the image of the statue wrapped in its long brown dress.

'Do you have something strong to offer me? An old liqueur, a little whisky?'

I went to the bar set into our glass display cabinet. I found only the dregs of an old bottle of walnut liqueur, since the drinks had not been replenished since the death of Giorgio de Paolis. I gave the priest his little glass, and again I asked him what happened to the statue's dress.

'I found that it was worn at the elbows and the hips as the result of pressure from the plaster, an unexpected wear and tear that caught me off guard.'

'How could that be?'

'The damp that lingers in the church and that winter's rains. I cannot help but blame the rains.'

'But barely a year has passed since it was last repaired. Damp takes more time than that to act,' I said, feeling extremely sure of myself.

There was a pause, during which the priest finally lit his cigar and took four or five good big puffs. Then he started to speak again.

'You see, I must tell you that the dress was never repaired. When, a year ago, the gold disappeared from the statue, it didn't take much to convince the parishioners that it had been required in order to buy a new dress. It really wasn't necessary to start giving explanations that they would not have understood. So, by giving the fabric a quick brush and the strings a bit of a wax, the old dress was made as good as new and no one noticed a thing. They're not the brightest people, hereabouts.'

'And what became of the gold?' I asked.

'Good question! It's a mystery, my dear, a genuine mystery. But the stash will soon be recovered, you'll see; these poverty-stricken folk are too fearful.'

'By which you mean?'

'That they will go without anything, even the merest farthings that they possess, to put themselves back within the statue's orbit of protection.'

'You seem to be mocking them, but I have heard you encouraging donations in a powerful and practised voice.'

'Of course, of course. It is my duty to encourage. To quote from the scripture: *Give and it shall be given, because the measure with which you measure will be measured against*

you too. And again: *Lay not up for yourselves treasures on earth,
where moth and rust destroy and where thieves break in and steal,
but lay up for yourselves treasures in heaven, where neither moth
nor rust corrupts, and where thieves do not break through and
steal.* Is that enough for you?'

'These people have no treasures, but they do have
moths and rust in abundance. And yet they must give what
they have, whenever they can.'

'But there is nothing that comes from the heart, my
dear girl. There is always a mean interest lurking underneath. For example, in one particular year one individual,
poor in funds, gave the statue a gold necklace weighing no
less than three ounces; a donation that could be explained
only in light of certain filthy practices that the fellow
indulged in once his wife had recovered from cervical
arthritis. Another year, a woman publicly cursed the dead
relations of her sister-in-law; by way of reply, the sister-in-
law put a curse on her, using a lock of hair that she herself
had torn from her during an argument. That year both
women felt the need to donate a nice big bracelet to the
statue: they bought it together, dividing the cost, because
they both had corruption in their soul. I could go on, but
the examples would show only how their faith was based
on nothing but their wretchedness.'

'You shouldn't insult them. They are a flock, isn't that
so? Your flock. At least that's what you call from the pulpit,
filling the whole space of the church. You should really be
the one to guide them.'

'And what do you know about anything, my dear girl?
These people enjoy being under the heel: you can feel them
stiffening, turning into a piece of wood, but you will never
see them taking offence; if you just crush them a little

more they simply give in. Tell them to come and they will come. Tell them to move and they move. To leave and they leave. You can flay them alive and they won't notice; their brains are closed, they are obtuse.'

'And yet you take from them the flour and poultry of which they deprive themselves to fill your sacristy, you even take their legacies and their donations. And I don't need to quote the book of Deuteronomy to remind you that priests are forbidden from owning property and receiving bequests.'

'Quote, quote away! They donate to secure the safety of their souls, certainly not for me. But now leave me in peace, because I need to reflect: you may unintentionally have given me an idea for repairing the dress.'

'May I ask what it is?'

'Provisions, girl, the big bags of flour and chestnuts, walnuts and eggs with which they fill my sacristy. Enough to feed an army, which will soon rot in the damp of the church. But I have put the wine and oil in safety. So this is the big idea. I will organise a festival with those products, and everyone will be able to buy them as they wish, paying for them with a slight *supplement* above and beyond the current prices because those goods have been in the church for months, and the blessing of the Holy Mass has fallen upon them every day.'

'Oh, that's wonderful!' I exclaimed, unable to contain myself. 'So this big idea of yours is a fraud. You want to put these people in the position of buying back the very things they've deprived themselves of to give to you, at a hiked-up price?'

'Fraud, you call it? A notional fraud. You'll see how grateful they are. And in the end what do they need?

A fistful of consecrated grain to scatter in the fields and infect future harvests with good fortune? They want oil, blessed oil to ease their headaches so that they don't need to visit the doctor. They would give up their lives for half a dozen eggs with the whiff of blessing to fortify their sickly children better than the meat they can't afford.'

'So you will have balanced the global economy in your favour to avoid having to contribute to it again,' I interrupted him, because by that point enough was enough.

'What do you know about anything? I'm saying they'll be happy to reacquire some things that have been so close to the *infinite*. I'm sure that they will feel amply reimbursed for the horrors inflicted by the *finite* that only chases them away like dogs. I, for my part, will acquire a new dress for the statue, like the old one but undamaged. And now leave me alone: I need to define the details of the idea.'

One could only wonder how the statue might have felt at that juncture, extremely alone and with little pride in its destiny. A question that Don Basilio didn't even touch upon, immediately immersing himself as he did in the definition of his big idea. I left the room. Outside, in spite of the darkness and the rain, it was spring, as evidenced by the first flies that were starting to circle the street lights. Everything that is reborn in springtime, I said to myself, coincides here with those things that are never reborn. I hated the great immortal peace that, as era followed era, constantly forced men into the same places as before, always the same places. Right before me I had the last links of a chain that went back down the generations to the origin of servitude. The Church, even the Church, barely gave it a thought, and left those stillborn people to soak in their cold sweat; its reign was clearly of this world, and hence it was touched by time, which rendered it variable and vain. It was not least for that reason that I abandoned the cloister and the dress.

I slipped into bed, tiptoeing in the dark, but it was an uneasy darkness, broken by the filaments of light that passed through the curtains. It's springtime, I thought, but then my breast was frozen by a mind of winter. I heard the almost metallic sound of the claws of the dog striking the cobblestones. I rose from my bed to gesture it to stop. I couldn't understand why, even though it had a kennel, it never went inside it, not even when the rain was hammering down. The fact was that old Gideon, out there, had always known something that I was disconcerted to discover: with the high forehead and attitude of someone who maintains a certain purity, he asked me, 'How do you get blood from a stone?' 'I can't,' I replied. 'You can't,' he said.

Marcello

'It's a big day today,' I said to my mother when she told me that Estella wouldn't be coming with us to the new town.

'A big day?' she replied. 'We're about to leave our house unwillingly. Does that seem like a big day to you?'

'She won't be coming with us, and she made the decision all by herself. It's a good cause for celebration.'

My mother looked at me as one might look at a cockroach.

'Estella decided to stay in the old village, demonstrating great courage. She will stay in our house and be its guardian,' she said, and brought her fists to her hips.

'She will be buried by the landslide.'

'That won't happen.'

'How do you know? The order to leave the village was imperative, and she runs a serious risk if she stays.'

'Nothing will happen to Estella,' she cut in, and I noticed a strange concentration on her face. Then, turning around abruptly, she left the room.

I can't say on what basis this prediction of my mother's was founded, or what the source of her divinatory arrogance might have been. She had always had curious presentiments, exacerbated by her unshakeable and almost maniacal devotion to the dead. In any case I wasn't interested in finding out. I was twenty-four years old, and I was about to open up new paths for myself, infinite possibilities. All around me there was a general hustle and bustle, a collective delirium along the road that led from the old village to the new. Old men growling, women growling, children growling too. The yokels, with their frozen-potato faces, had decided to go and stand outside their houses:

some of them were happy because they were going to have a new house; others wept as they caressed the walls of the hovel that they would have to abandon.

As for me, I gathered positive energy and drew optimism from the change: there would no longer be a house of rage and deprivation, and, more importantly, there would no longer be Estella, whose memory I would wrap in a rag and hang from the ceiling, and leave it there to insult like the body of a traitor who had tried to hang himself.

I will never see her again, I said to myself, I will not see her wandering lugubriously around the house of which she has taken charge. My heart was all a-tremble and seemed to want to weep to free itself from the sensations that besieged it. It's over, I repeated to myself. Her eyes, those sharp, narrow eyes, will never again settle on me. Her pale face and her hair, that stupid hair, will never again accidentally brush against me.

I felt a huge desire to strike her again, as I did from time to time when she least expected it. Then, however, I was swept by a sense of great tenderness, as if several weights had been lifted from me: at last, I was about to free myself from her and from my obsessions, which largely coincided. Estella hadn't died as I had hoped in the eight years of our cohabitation, but now I knew that she was merely a word that I could do without.

The most consistent exodus was seen from the 1960s onwards, even though the first arrangements to clear the precarious village dated back to the turn of the century.

At the end of the nineteenth century, the alleyways of the village had filled with the water that had surged powerfully down the hill, forming streams and puddles that ate away at the foundations of the houses. At those points where the terrain fell away as if yielding to pressure, water collected in ditches from which it was unable to escape. The same thing also happened in the big square, which turned into a malarial swamp. Only the elm tree seemed unaffected: the water swirled around it, murmuring a sorrowful song, but it did not weaken its roots, which remained intact, or its branches, still stirred by the frivolous wind.

The Alentesi went on visiting the square, and drawing water from the public well a little way down from the square, as stubbornly as they knocked down the frail walls of their damp dwellings and tirelessly rebuilt them. They became accustomed to the instability of the ground on which their lives were played out, as if accepting something ineluctable that could not be controlled.

Besides, the landslide had never been the worst thing: the worst thing was poverty, which had always been there, constant and invincible, just like the landslide. And in fact it seemed as if the two things moved together, as if together they were acting out a dance whose steps the Alentesi had learned very well. The village was disintegrating and its inhabitants were falling into debt because of the perpetual losses, the fallen walls, the collapsing roofs that needed rebuilding at least once a year. They were training, in short, not to pay attention to a quiet kind of earthquake that flowed beneath their feet.

In the year when the de Paolis family also left along with Peppa, the mayor had been unshakeable: the move was to take place as quickly as possible so as not to incur expenses for the disinterment of corpses from the wreckage, much greater than the sums requested for the move. In spite of that, many families preferred to stay in the old village, especially those who lived above the square, where the houses had been damaged only slightly by the landslide. Those who planned to move to the new village were the well-to-do families – who would be able to build houses even more sumptuous than the ones they had lived in before – and the very poor, who had been stripped of everything by the moving earth. That was the case for the Paudice family – husband, wife and an only son – who lived in the valley, in one of the steepest areas. One night, while the three were sleeping in the only room on the upstairs floor of their house, a beam very close to the bed gave way. The mother managed to grab both her son and her husband by an arm, and together they climbed over the undamaged part of the roof. At that moment, two chests of grain happened to tilt together, blocking the hole in the floor. The three managed not to fall, but they lost everything and there was no way to rebuild the house. They too moved to a new village, as soon as they could.

I stayed in the de Paolis house, with the big building made of memories to keep me company, a building that grew bigger by the year and, when the last families left, was finally terrifying.

For a few years I had the company of the families whose houses were as yet unthreatened by the landslide, and the graveyard, which soon became a pasture for stray dogs. Some widows remained, among them Libera Forti, who often came to visit me. She suffered from strange accidents, lured by the same mysteries that had lured her father. She often suffered attacks of uncontrollable laughter and just as often collapsed into fearful sobs. She constantly repeated a nonsense rhyme that might once have been a prayer; I worked out many years later – only after she began to take part in the dinners in that house – the private meaning that that litany held for her. Libera Forti had the faiths and illusions of a poor madwoman, but she was not mad. A stifled cry seemed to accompany her wherever she went, and that had been the case since the day when the bodies of her husband and son had been brought home to her, crushed by a load of hay bales, before being laid on two planks of wood. Libera never looked in the mirror, and if by some misadventure she happened to glimpse herself in a pane of glass she fell to the ground, defeated. She might not have been in the first flush of youth, but she was still in relatively good health. Her old age was due less to her advanced years than to her appearance, which had adapted prematurely to the closure of her heart. As if to demonstrate this, she wandered around in ambiguous attire that looked more like the soiled dress of a housewife than mourning clothes. Worst of all, though, was her hair: a few sparse locks that sprouted from her head amidst self-inflicted bumps and scabs. Nonetheless, on many of my gloomy wakeful evenings I found her, of all people, to be a companion with whom I could recall the past, not mine alone but that of the village, which remained clear in my mind and in hers as well.

That was why, when she disappeared – perhaps swallowed up by the hole in the Angel's Grotto – I felt my loneliness to be all the more inconsolable, destined to grow by the day, vulnerable to regret and filled with gullibility.

By the time this house too began to collapse on top of me, one rustle of plaster after another, I was already exhausted and spending my evenings on my own, no longer wanting to know what precise moment in time I was living in. I asked for nothing; I sat by the walls, which gave off their hiss of life, and asked for nothing. I was waiting, that's true, but I was aware of how pointless that waiting was, because nothing could come but voices, those voices consigned to an eternity of silence, like the event that had never occurred, as if they had never belonged to anyone, as if that anyone had been no one, a pure and precise nothing within the dust of archive dust. But how could they not have existed, I said to myself, if they had built those walls and dwelt within them?

It was only thus that I managed not to fall into the trap of victimhood, succumbing to abandonment. Eventually, every poor thing began to speak to me, to make a racket within the play of memory, because will alone was never enough for anyone.

Movements and faces returned to life one by one, and each time I have been delighted to find them so pretty and so polite. It takes time and a certain detachment to decide which to bring back to life and which not. The ones that came to me in dreams, of course – they have stayed. As to the rest, we'll see. And it doesn't count if they are hidden behind a door or the cracks of a supporting wall, with their sly little cries: 'I was there and she didn't see me.' Honesty, my dear dead ones, honesty, or at least a little respect for those of us who are only just dead enough.

Part Two

Waiting

Forse un mattino andando in un'aria di vetro,
arida, rivolgendomi, vedrò compirsi il miracolo:
il nulla alle mie spalle, il vuoto dietro
di me, con un terrore di ubriaco.

Poi come s'uno schermo, s'accamperanno di gitto
alberi case colli per l'inganno consueto.
Ma sarà troppo tardi; ed io me n'andrò zitto
tra gli uomini che non si voltano, col mio segreto.

Perhaps one morning walking in dry, glassy air,
turning, I will see the miracle occur:
the nothing behind me, the void within
me, with a drunk's terror.

Then as on a screen
trees houses hills will suddenly appear in the usual illusion.
But it will be too late; and I will walk on silently
among the men who do not turn, with my secret.

Eugenio Montale, *Forse un mattino andando*
in un'aria di vetro
(Perhaps one morning walking in dry, glassy air)

Estella

I clearly remember the slow passing of the years in Alento, their soft tranquillity. The men approaching one another without gesture or exclamation. Lame pigeons, forced to stand on a single, rheumatic foot; pigeons with wings that they never used, which served as target practice for mobs of unruly youths.

One after the other, as I see them, the decades consist of frames connected by subdued impoverishment, by condemnation to moribund life. But the years have passed as they must.

It was in the course of that year, memorable for its exodus, that Marcello also left. One day when it was already autumn, as one could chiefly tell by the coagulated light, on that day he left this house, the house that was truly his even though I had lived there as if it were my own; he left me as he had found me – in the sturdiest skirt I possessed, my hair hanging loosely but only for my own delight; he abandoned me, in fact, even though we had never been together. From that moment he granted me one visit only, once a year, for the November dinner, and a rancorous glare, a kind of prehensile look from the new village, in a stubborn attempt to forget.

In the years during which we lived together we had lacked strength. Too young to give each other miraculous answers to questions that we weren't even aware of, we made one another cold. Obviously we didn't talk about it, and perhaps – definitely – we were assailed by doubts – or I was, at least. In fact he was seething away, like puddle water when the earth beneath is hot. I waited. It isn't clear even now what I was waiting for. At any rate it didn't take much for us to part, even though I subsequently made no effort to be with him, even for only a day. He kept his life elsewhere, and I didn't want to be in that elsewhere. I never actually went to his new house, not even when Ada de Paolis died three years after they moved; not even when Peppa left, weary of the new situation to which she had never managed to accustom herself.

I often found myself wondering how we would one day be reunited. There was nothing substantial about the distance that had been created between us, given that his new house stood only a few miles from this one. And yet that distance always seemed to be unbridgeable, so much so that I cannot pause for more than a moment below his window when I go to the new village to buy provisions. Not from unease, not that. It is only that what has remained unshakeable and unconditional within me is the conviction that nothing must happen between us. As if I could only impose a reasonable order on my life in the absence of someone else. As if, exhausted by waiting, I constantly had to recreate that dissolving shell of mine, that little closed-off world in which I am reborn and die each time. I convinced myself that I had protected Marcello, keeping him far from my dangerous heart, but in fact I was protecting myself and my feigned quiescence. At the same time, I thought I had an infinite amount of time and that sooner or later I would recover, that we would see each other again tomorrow, perhaps calling ourselves by different names, and that I had to leave everything as it was.

Now that my life is governed by memories, now that the house is collapsing, on that terrible day when I thought that I would finally be ready, I know that I am also ready to die. Oh, if only a brief message would come. Oh, if only it would come!

Instead, what I am left with is the village, with its magical imposture. Here I rummage about in the evenings in search of the coming dawn. I am forever entering the houses that stand open, their windows ajar as if the former inhabitants are due to return at any moment, and the cobwebs stick to my face. In that desolation I see forming before me the images of a strange and summonable vision. I see all sides at once, and the dead who passed through them, all the ages of those who lived there. The mothers with their children in their arms, heavy as rocks; the old women, constricted in their eternal mourning weeds; the fathers, their bodies besieged by terror because living among the mountains did not keep them from poverty.

I walk on the shifting bricks and go into the kitchens, still with their necklaces of chilli peppers hanging from the ceiling, kitchens where people had just eaten, with hearths that smelled of soot, blackened by the smoke which, on evenings of twisting winds, blew back inside and filled the rooms. One of the houses has the floor of an upper storey suspended in the air, with only a scaffolding of ivy holding it up as best it can. Further on there is a house that is almost intact, with cracked walls bearing traces of an old climbing rose, and beside the hearth there is a basket, still full of wood. There are weeds everywhere, in the old vegetable gardens, growing up the walls. Nature's rage has also been unleashed against the old shops, which are devoured by encroaching plants; the blacksmith's forge is blocked off by a wall of moss that obstructs any approach. And look at the cellars: they resemble sarcophagi with the lumps of concrete that have fallen from the walls to form canopic jars.

In the dust of these ruins, in this time-scattered dust, I can make out faces, objects, hair left among the rocks, shoelaces entwined with the ribs of leaves, the fissured joints and chairs and ephemeral clothes. One word at a time, while I have life, I will sketch out the story of this village. Starting with the story of the Forti family.

Their house stands in the twisted alleyway just before the road that leads up to the mountain. There is a pergola on the front of the house, supported by a few grey pillars. In its time it acted as an excellent shaded passageway, filled as it was with vine leaves and bunches of grapes that hung on all sides. One fine day, Cola Forti sat down under that pergola and never moved again, his legs becalmed, eyes as tearful as those of a dog that has ceased to run even in its sleep. Every now and again he would receive a visit from Libera, his only daughter, visits that she paid without conviction; shorter each time, in fact, until she resolved never to go there again.

The story of that father and his life suspended in circles of libertarian ideas; the story of that daughter who carried around her own constraints; a whole mixture of faces and memories that have lingered in my mind, that have taken root there and rob me of sleep, but I don't hold it against them because I have only one desire: to retain their company.

Cola Forti

It was on one evening in September 1935 that Libera Forti, her heart in turmoil, cried that she was not in a state to get married, and no one had ever heard her speak so loudly. It was not that she lacked anything required for matrimonial life, but she could not bear the plan that her mother had drawn up for her, a plan in which she ended up sadly languishing in the arms of Michelangelo il Guercio, 'the Squinter', a slob with hair growing out of his nose and ears.

Everyone was startled, particularly Apollonia, who had certainly not brought a daughter into the world so that she might rebel like that against decisions that had been taken irrevocably. The neighbours were startled too, and the aunts, and even the eighty-year-old grandmother who had never wished for a shrewish old maid of a granddaughter.

Only Cola, from the depths of his darkness, was not startled, and nor did he think of uniting his voice with his wife's. In fact he seemed almost on the point of being moved when he recognised in his daughter's fury the fire of his own that had been extinguished too soon.

He had always been an idealist, a fanatic. His eyes filled with tears when he spoke of the oppressed, of the marginalised, his fists raised to heaven. A great heart, even a noble one, but Apollonia didn't know what to do with it because she had never missed an opportunity to remind him of one very simple thing: that ideals had never put food on anyone's table, and that they too, besides, were also oppressed and marginalised. So much so that a daughter married to a good worker – the minor flaw of uncouthness aside – was without a doubt to be preferred to a spinster daughter. All the more so in that Libera was over thirty and no one before Guercio had asked for her hand. And besides, Guercio – Squinter – was not the poor fellow's real name, only the sobriquet attached to the family by peasant wit, a stupid nickname that went back down the generations; the family's actual surname was Riccio – Curly – which created a different effect altogether.

Quite honestly, Apollonia was by now convinced that ignorance made ideas much clearer than school primers, and she was in a position to say so, given that fate had landed her with a husband who had never brought a cent into the house even though he could read and write better than many a lettered man. What was more, since in the Forti household there was no limit to how bad things could get, the persistent rumours of subversion surrounding Cola will certainly not have helped.

She was aware, as was he, that printing work did not fall from the sky like rain, and it was only thanks to the intervention of his nephew, a staunch young fascist, that the printer had agreed to take on Cola as his assistant.

They both knew that after the last elections, even though the village had proved its strength of character by voting in the Fascist Party, everyone, particularly in their own homes, had their suspicions about who might have been responsible for the opposing votes. It would have been better, a hundred times better, if he had been sent somewhere to get his ideas in order. But because in the village not even the fascists were as rigorous as they might have been elsewhere, a layabout like Cola was left peacefully at home.

Now, if he had had the merest hint of good sense he would have hung on to that job, given that there were no others, rather than showing himself for what he was: a rambunctious loudmouth and nothing else.

Cola, for his part, didn't trouble in the slightest about his wife's concerns, because he didn't really quite understand them. As anyone could see, his job in the printworks meant working for a boss who could afford to live by exploiting the labour of others. The prospect of earning his daily bread by working for bloodsuckers, and fascist bloodsuckers to boot, was never going to be to his liking. Had he been able to line them up in his mind, they would have been nothing but a crowd of postcard moustaches, a triumphal procession of hollow heads, wasted breath, fat bellies and neuroses, surrounded by a mob of beggar-folk ready at any moment to turn themselves into dependable hangmen. He couldn't bring himself to feel grateful for this new job unless, reversing the perspective, he allowed himself to see the Linotype, with all its cranks and matrices, the rotary press, the paper and even the ink, as his property, thus making the finished product the result of his own labour.

Such ideas might have seemed ludicrous, and perhaps they were, but they would have ceased to be so if millions of people in the world had adopted them. Ideas based on equality of working conditions; solidarity their beacon, liberty their goal. Ideas that proposed the radical abolition of the domination of one human being by another. Who could not have wished for such a thing?

When Cola had attempted to persuade his wife to join in with his vision, she had merely snorted and rolled her eyes. What his wife failed to understand was that he lived in the future. The present did not concern him. On the other hand, this was precisely why he had not achieved a great deal in his life, lest he be crushed by the weight of preserving things in which he had not the slightest interest.

He had attempted to explain to her that the future would make her petty concerns disappear in a puff of smoke, but Apollonia had always replied with an explosion of laughter. He had therefore given up telling her the rest, because there was nothing in her empty head but twilight, the moment before the darkest night, a genuine simulacrum of death.

'So you want me to work in the printworks like a slave?' he asked her one evening, when Apollonia least expected it.

'What sort of question is that? I suppose you don't want to eat every day?' she replied, caressing her mauve-coloured lace dress, which had long since lost its lace and also much of its mauve.

Cola hesitated for a moment before replying: it was clear that his wife was speaking in a voice that combined a thousand others, all the voices of other people. Even her devotion to fascism, saying yes not only with her head but also with her spirit, convinced as she was that the land reclamation planned by the fascists would add a great deal to their meagre savings, was proof once again of a limited and susceptible mind. He felt sorry for her.

'If you're so keen I'll do it, but on my own terms,' he replied.

'Don't talk to me about terms, I don't want to hear a word about it,' she said to him in a tone that brooked no reply. Then, before leaving him with the sense of guilt that he deserved, she looked at him with eyes full of commiseration. 'I would love to know what it is that drives you so insane,' she said and, with a deep sigh, hurried from the room because she didn't want to be subjected to another of his delirious rants.

The problem was that Cola had already made up his mind. Since that moment he had been certain of only one thing: if moss never grew on a rolling stone, he had every intention of seeing to it that the stone rolled vigorously.

He felt very sorry for those apathetic characters who lived in the darkness of resignation. At the tavern in the evening, they passed before him one by one, drowning in wine their hatred for State and Church – a pairing to blame for their empty bellies; but they all drifted past as slowly and inexorably as their uneventful days. Sometimes he surprised himself by giving them a sideways glance, while they didn't bat an eyelid. It was as if they had dissolved, vanished from the earth on the very day of their birth. In spite of that, they perpetuated their own image in their children, endlessly repeating themselves. What kind of human race had he fallen into? When he returned home he sometimes found himself stopping to stare at the street, which seemed to be empty but was in fact full of dead people blindly waving their arms around, lining up with the despairing slowness of those who have never really been alive. The idea of his country's innocence would have made farmyard animals laugh. No, he felt no compassion for people who succumbed to apathy.

The next morning, with his straw hat plonked firmly on his head, he turned up at the printworks, without the slightest intention of laying out the pages of the newspaper on the bench as he had been asked to do. For the stone to roll, a slope was required. What that stone was, Cola could not have said. He knew that it was not to be confused with a marble or a button that had fallen from a jacket – in fact, it was better to pull one's buttons off to distinguish oneself from all those conformists. The stone was exceptional, he knew that, a prodigy that could end up in the furthest place imaginable, or even in the sea, and that was enough.

He thought that he might be able to start by using the articles in the *Gazzetta*, by adding imperceptible modifications, innocent-looking amendments, before sending them to the press.

The first opportunity arose two weeks later when the article came in announcing the appointment and installation in office of the new magistrate. He subjected it to a detailed analysis and, like distillate in the alembic, the text that emerged the following day corresponded to the original in every respect but for a tiny final supplement:

This Magistracy has been placed under the governance of Geco Paolo Antonio, from the town of Cosenza.

He is a young and courageous civil servant, and he has already won general sympathy and admiration.

He is a fascist by pure and true conviction.

We give him a warm welcome and wish him the best of luck with the job.

Similar warm wishes go to the Cancelliere Sig. Fenuca Giasone, he too a young and greatly appreciated civil servant. Unimpeachable in the exercise of his functions and pleasant in manner, he too is welcomed with sympathy and admiration.

Under the direction of its new Magistrate Sig. Geco, the Magistracy has regained the promptness that restores it to the degree of importance that it has always had.

And greetings also to the most excellent Maresciallo Sig. Improta Lillino, who, during the brief period in which he has been in command of

the Station of the Carabinieri, RR CC, has enjoyed
the esteem that befits an honest and appreciated
servant of the state.

To all of the above our deepest best wishes,
trusting that we will see them *in caelis*, as they
deserve, at the first possible opportunity.

Some of his colleagues were unsettled by this conclusion,
with its hint of bad luck, but Cola explained that this was
an elegant Latin phrase, which should be read as a wish that
they reach the most supreme heights, close to heaven.

Over the days that followed, everyone read that Dr
Romildo Lesi had acquired a most elegant OM motor car,
the first that had been seen *flatulating* in these parts, and
that the lawyer Alberico Florio, the courageous militia lieu-
tenant of Alento, was moving from Valva to Castelnuovo
di Conza in his capacity as chief magistrate and, although
everyone was pleased with his new role, the *Vulvas* already
regretted his passing.

Reproaches began raining down on Cola, almost falling
into his lap. He felt proud of being seen in a poor light. Any
disappointment in his regard filled him with calm. He lived
in the future, and the present concerned him not in the
slightest.

It was with the same gratified feeling of triumph that
he presented the news of the return of Count Augusto de
Marinis, who, after a year's residence in Rome – where he
had acquired a splendid apartment in a luxurious building
near Villa Torlonia – was returning to the village for a brief
holiday in his new automobile with the lovely Signorina
Gemma, his daughter and second-born, and a maid. The
estimable Signora Giulia and the gracious Filiberto had

travelled ahead by train with the other maid. *To the esteemed Dottore and his distinguished family* the newspaper offered *the best wishes for a pleasant stay followed by an excellent imminent demise.*

While the hands of the clock turned with inexorable slowness, the stone had begun to roll in the right direction, and the more it rolled, the more convinced Cola became that he would soon feel the warm breeze of the future on his face. Nor could his wife, uneasy as she was, sap his enthusiasm when he said that without moss, sooner or later the stone would roll into the river and drown.

What could she know from the depths of her mental twilight? She too was one of those who were barely alive, living without really knowing how to do so, like rats gnawing at logs.

As he stood looking down on the surging and uncertain waves of the future, Cola opened his eyes wide and gazed into the distance. Naive observers said that he was delusional, that he expected nothing from life. He replied with a shrug: such people's existences were meaningless, frittered away on fruitless activities that kept them from truly acting.

The stone had begun to roll, allowing Cola to yield to the impulse to push it further. The opportunity to do so arose when it came to printing the news item concerning a successful soirée for the benefit of the fascist group Opera Nazionale Balilla.

Yesterday, before a select audience, in the Municipal Theatre used as the seat of the Comitato Balilla, presided over by its tireless President Captain Oscar Contenuto, a magnificent show was given, with the performance of D'Annunzio's *Fiammata*.

The performers, impeccable in their form and enunciation, were given long and spontaneous applause.

The student Antonio di Ferdinando Vigori played the part of Colonnello Felt with the warmth of a truly great actor. No less evocative was Signorina Laura Iovine in the role of Monica, holding the stage in a manner hitherto unique in an amateur performance.

She revealed herself in all her intelligence and performed with a truly magnificent degree of self-confidence.

The other members of the cast were excellent.

In short, they all deserved the warmest congratulations from the audience, who gave the amateurs an impressive *ovulation* at the end.

The performance was held to raise funds for the municipal committee of the Opera Nazionale Balilla and brought in a considerable amount.

The amateur actors were then offered food, drink and flowers, which were appreciated for their colour and perfume not least by the children, who were not allowed to enter the building and stayed outside to look in through the windows.

The response was collective outrage, a chorus of protest, condemnation for Cola. The authorities shouted loudly, and the printer worried that his own time was up; he soon announced, however, that Cola Forti would be leaving his position with immediate effect, and the shouting subsided.

Dragged abruptly from his sleep as if by the rattle of

gunfire, Cola was obliged to realise that the stone had indeed rolled, but not in the direction he had intended.

He understood this even more clearly when even the anarchist Massenzio told him that his stubborn bid to straighten twisted timber was pointless, like his efforts to clear the many puddles in the village streets. And Cola felt a familiar pang in his belly when his friend spoke to him of the future but as a dream, as something entirely imaginary. Now, in this climate, he opted to take refuge so as not to run any pointless risks, risks that could only be harmful.

'You carefully prepare a loaf,' Massenzio said to him, 'and then the oven burns it up with an unexpected blaze. What do you end up with? A black crust. You will have only crusts of bad bread that no one will be able to eat, not even you.'

Cola felt like one of those stray dogs that he saw passing along the street five or six times at night, going faster each time.

Certainly, he would have difficult arguments, he wanted to say to him. Mistakes would be made, how could they not be? But seeking shelter now would mean lowering himself to a first compromise, then a second, then a third. He would still be standing at the end, but on what?

The pair looked at one another. After that, they said goodbye for a second time and nothing else, because they had nothing more to say to each other, not even in the name of the old ideas of a past that might never have existed.

Cola felt the desire to walk towards the sea on the horizon, apparently a relatively short distance away. He felt as if he had found at that moment a point towards which he could advance. He considered that it was a reasonable distance away and began walking as if towards a mirage.

All that he had to do was not turn around, but that was easy because it was the thought of the future that impelled him forward: the carts, the men hurrying to finish their days, the cattle chewing the cud by the roadside. Everything vanished again as soon as it appeared.

He thought of the surging waves, the beaches of fine sand ready to caress his feet as he walked towards the future. He turned his mind towards it again as he headed quickly downhill, because the sea was change, openness, the way to the future.

As soon as he reached the bottom, covered in sweat and with his knees inflamed, he looked around and began to fret. At the furthest point that his eye could reach he could see only a few scraps of field, some green, some yellow. He went on walking, but froze when he reached a parapet from which the sea could no longer be seen, lost in a mass of rocky earth and worse.

Stretching his body until it was almost level with the top of a tree, he seemed still to be able to see a patch of water in the distance, with the sun setting behind it. He looked again and all he could see was the pathetic strip of a canal in which an old woman was washing sheets.

There was no sea. He felt a kind of terror. Shadows were already falling and in front of him Cola had nothing, a glassy air, and behind him hills that seemed to have appeared out of nowhere, mountains, caves creating the usual illusion.

It was then that he understood that the place was lost forever.

He remained motionless until evening, like a dog without a master. He didn't stir until the darkness was total. Then he got to his feet. Then he turned back towards Alento.

Then he felt cold.

His fierce faith in the future had been the basis of his hopes, his determination to live. Now he was left with only one clear sensation, the pain that lashed him from within.

He quickly passed through the vegetable gardens that appeared in front of him, treading carelessly even on cultivated soil: contemptible, utterly contemptible, even though it had seeds growing in it. Then he took the path leading into the forest, and like a dog following its nose, he found himself at home in time for dinner.

He didn't want to talk, so he kept his suffering to himself, hoping that by making some kind of effort he would be able to turn it into something else. From time to time, of course, he would still be seized by spasms of impatience, but he could deduce nothing from them: the important thing was to stay alert and catch them as they appeared.

At table he announced that from now on he would not be leaving the house, and asked to have a rocking chair set up under the pergola, because that was where he was going to spend the rest of his days, in a silent stillness that his thoughts could not penetrate. His only companion would be a bottle of grappa. Otherwise he would feel neither hot nor cold, and he would no longer be hot or cold himself.

So a few months later, when Apollonia announced that she was marrying their daughter off to Squinter, the great worker, after his initial dismay Cola didn't stir, he didn't say a word. He didn't move even when Libera threw herself at his feet, begging him to allow her to stay in the family home.

'How can you consent to something like that?' she asked tearfully, resting her cheek against her father's knees.

'Beware, my daughter, beware,' Cola replied in almost a whisper.

'What should I beware of?'

'Of the piles of rubble that trickle down the mountain with the first September rains. The stones without moss – ask your mother – end up in the river and drown.'

Baffled, Libera shook him with her arms as if to bring him back to life from his apparent death: the freedom with which he had filled her head, and the future, and all that talk of the oppressed and the marginalised. Was she not perhaps oppressed herself? It was at that moment that Cola seemed to be almost on the brink of an emotion, recognising in his daughter certain impulses that were familiar to him. Then, with a crisp gesture of his hand, he sent her away, as if mistaking her for a fly. Then he started rocking again. Then nothing.

Libera Forti

The conclusion that Libera Forti reached – some time after
the celebration of her marriage to Squinter – was that
waiting was the only option.

She had tried everything she could think of to avert the
wedding, she had even threatened to run away and become
a nun, but Apollonia had refused to listen to reason, and her
father hadn't said a word.

The wedding was held in December, one morning when
the wind was swelling the dark green tips of the pine trees
more than usual. The couple were wed in the darkness
of the church, which was softened only by three candles,
while outside the day's last rays were swiftly turning to
night. Their closest relatives were there, a dozen of them,
and there was no music. The ceremony was followed by a
frugal meal in the village tavern and that was all.

Libera wore a mid-length grey dress, while Squinter
was dressed in a black suit in line with the fashion of the
time. The bride's only accessory was a velvet ribbon around
her wrist to which was pinned a sprig of heather with
beautiful pink buds.

The original intention was for the wedding ring to be
Apollonia's own gold one, a kind of handover, a rite of
motherhood that would be her final and most accomplished
gesture. In fact it was a little iron circle stamped with the
words *Gold for the Fatherland*.

As chance would have it, it was during these days that
Apollonia had donated her wedding ring to the campaign
against the blockade on Italy after the Italian invasion of
Ethiopia. A sacrifice that she could very easily have spared
herself, given that she had a daughter to marry and the

household savings were far from lavish, but after the events in which her husband had involved himself – only through his boorish fanaticism – Apollonia had convinced herself that the least she could do was demonstrate her dedication to the needs of the Fatherland. All the more so in that the certificate of receipt for the donation was very large and could be seen hanging on the living-room wall, with the 'Fascist Party in Combat' letterhead at the top.

So that morning, Libera's hand was darkened with an iron ring that bore the weight of her mother's sacrifice, not her own; she put it on herself because Squinter, at the moment when it came to taking her finger, was wiping his forehead and couldn't quite manage it.

In the evening, when the last relative had left, Libera realised that the man had taken a wife for his own satisfaction and for no other reason. In fact, after emptying himself in front of her of the piss that he had retained during the day, he set the chamber pot back down under the bed and, without a word, was on top of her even before she knew what was happening, merely indicating with a glance the bar on the headboard that she was supposed to hold on to. Libera felt a kind of nausea, but, clutching the bar with both hands, she felt the cold of the iron running through her, and it was like a fraternal touch, benign in its way. Then, when Squinter, almost prey to a kind of rage, turned her over like a sack and was on her again like a wild beast, Libera finally broke a tooth against the bar, a sign that nothing in this house, not even a bar, was going to be on her side.

When Squinter finished, he withdrew to his side of the bed and was asleep in five minutes, without a word to his wife. Libera wondered if he mightn't be dead, after the exertion of having her underneath him, but the sound of the corn husks rustling in the mattress indicated that he wasn't dead at all. She decided to get up and relieve her nerves, rubbing her frozen hands, her knees and her feet, which felt like marble. She yielded to the impulse to look at herself in the mirror, only to tell herself that she wasn't dead. She looked at herself and no, she wasn't dead, because she was moving and standing upright, while dead people lie horizontally. She wasn't alive either, because her face was only a vague shape in the darkness, reduced to a mere shadow. Still, she felt the cold of the floor rising from her feet, a further indication that she wasn't dead, but then again neither was she quite alive. She felt something else coming from the floor. She looked down. It was as if some sort of pebble had got caught under the sole of her right foot. She sat down and lifted her foot. She was startled to realise that the tooth she had lost a short time before had entered her flesh. She took it out, wiped her foot with the hem of her nightshirt and went to the bathroom. In the cabinet beside the wash basin there were some little glass bottles; she took one, filled it with spirits and put the tooth into it. Then, after sealing it, she put it back in the cabinet, resolving to keep it there forever.

As soon as she found herself in the bathroom, she thought of washing herself with vinegar to take away the terrible odour she thought she could smell on herself, and the stinging sensation between her legs, which felt like a wound.

Her clothes, the basin, her menstrual fluid, her bed in her old house – she wished she could keep it all intact, she wasn't born to get married, to share her bed with anyone, least of all like this.

A coming of age. Some things she knew, some things her mother had told her, small things that weren't entirely clear. The most grievous betrayal was that of her father, who had sent her to school, secondary school indeed, but to do what? And then there was that business about the sea, always the sea. Cola had once taken her to the beach, and she had seen it licking the land, the sea that everyone travels across, the sea and the sound of the water, the sea and its surging waves.

How many useless words still buzzed around in her head: the excitement of leaving, the unturned furrow of the future, the great relief of sunrise, the sooner-or-later with its cargo of waiting: the then that had never come. 'Don't marry, daughter of mine, explore, go elsewhere, don't settle for a man from the village, stuck and limited, and with the look of an old dog,' was what he had said. All lies. There were two questions she wished she could have asked the man who had betrayed her worst of all. Only two simple cursed things that she wanted to know. First (and she raised her thumb into the air, rotating it slightly as if her father were in front of her): was she going to end up like this because he had chosen to call her Libera, the free one? Second (and she put her thumb back in its place, now waving her index and middle finger in the air): why had he talked to her of the future, string-free and sunlit, if her own meant ending up on a bed of corn husks? She waited for a moment, as if the answers that she was waiting for, in the words she knew, the ones she had heard and cherished so often at home, might somehow detach themselves from the emptiness of the room. She thought them and rethought them, and nothing, all dead, one after the other, dropping abruptly to the ground like dying birds.

Now there were different words to learn, words that sounded like shingle retreating when a wave, encountering an obstacle, is halted and repelled. There were new, un-climbable walls, and the nocturnal cries of the owls. That was what she still had of her previous life, which was dying that night: a convulsive cry of death, along with a bar on a bedhead and a rustle of corn husks.

The lamp burned greedily in the room, with its vast wick that seemed to suck out every last molecule of air, but Libera couldn't deal with that now. In the middle of the night she felt the weight of every passing hour, a weight of old logs on her back. At last she fell asleep where she was, curled up in a corner of the room.

Early the next morning she was woken by a strip of light that had escaped the dungeon of the walls and touched her on the forehead. She got up from the floor with a plan. She would go and see Apollonia, who, in spite of the cruelty of some of her decisions, was still her mother, after all. There was a rapport between them that was somehow closer than affection, even though in her earliest childhood memories her mother's shadows passed over her like a cloud over puddles. Then she got herself ready, as if some-thing as yet unimagined might come out of this outing; she put on her flannel cloak, her hat and her gloves and headed home, because the paternal house was her home, not Squinter's hovel, which stank of piss and corn husks. What had seemed unthinkable even the evening before now seemed like a possibility. Her mother would be unhappy – the end of a marriage is always sad, but then she would understand and bring her back home, removing her, as a woman, from her late-night humiliations. 'Yes, yes!' she said to herself cheerfully with a smile that exposed her teeth, 'Mother will understand,' and she narrowed her eyes a little as she smiled.

When she was on the threshold of the house she waited for a moment, uncertain whether to knock, but then she went straight inside because she had never knocked on the door of her own house.

Apollonia was in the kitchen, pressing her fists into a dough of flour and water; outside, under the pergola, Cola was beginning his day, still swathed in the remnants of the morning mist.

'I need to speak to you,' she said to her mother as soon as she was standing in front of her.

'What are you doing here?' her mother asked without looking up, still pressing her fists into the dough with a ferocity that consumed all her strength.

'I can't stand it, I don't want to stay with that yokel who behaves like an animal.'

'Well, listen to the silly girl. What are you saying?'

'I don't want us to sleep together anymore. Look at me. I even lost a tooth last night.'

'These things happen.'

'These things happen?' Libera replied.

'One missing tooth is hardly the end of the world. It's still better than going out to water the fields at night, so many fields, so many nights, as I had to do to feed you while your father spouted nonsense.'

'How can you let a man treat me like that?' the girl stammered, struggling to believe that those words had just been uttered by the woman who had brought her into the world.

'These are fantasies that have come out of your own head. Humiliations are something else entirely. Having no food to put on the table because your husband can't afford any, while other houses are coming down with it, that's humiliation.'

'But what does that have to do with what happens in bed?'

'Oh, you're annoying me now. That's just how men are, you're not the first or the last it's happened to.'

'My father never treated you like that.'

'Maybe that's why your father never even made sure his family had bread on the table. You know what he was doing while I was out digging the fields? Talking. Talking about the oppressed people of the world.'

'My father has always been a dreamer, someone you could talk to for hours. Squinter hasn't said a word to me yet. Please don't make me go back to him.'

'Your husband is a great worker and he has south-facing land.'

'What do I care for south-facing land? Better to die of hunger if that's the price to pay.'

'You don't know what hunger is, that's why you talk like this when you'd be better off keeping your mouth shut. Your husband is a good man. He won't let you want for anything if you don't give him cause to be unhappy, you'll see. Now go home, I'm busy.'

Libera couldn't bear to hear any more of that. She hadn't found a safe haven in her mother, and nor would she find one in her father, who, in the end, would listen to her in his silent, passive way, which was all the more irritating for that. She left the house, which only a short while before she had so proudly proclaimed to be her own, and walked out into the lashing wind. There wasn't much to be done, she had no option but to leave, but where could she go?

She wondered why she wasn't a bird, who at that moment could have soared aloft, far above the dull throb of betrayal. But she wasn't, so she turned down the road and returned the way she had come.

That was the beginning of her life as a married woman. From then on, she would make Squinter's meals for him, wash Squinter's clothes, look after Squinter and make sure he was happy, especially at night. He was a great worker. He had a lot of land, ten dairy cows and several sheep. He wasn't poor, and they certainly wouldn't go hungry, even though he had more wrinkles than flesh. But what price was to be paid for avoiding poverty?

She would have to wait for winter to pass, because winter is when a man lies on top of his wife; in the spring there was work to be done in the fields, there was the hay harvest, there was lots of work and she would finally get her breath back.

In the evening she prayed in silence, kneeling in her nightshirt. She wasn't praying in reality, she was just moving her lips as if in prayer, hoping that her husband would notice and be intimidated. That, in fact, did not happen. Evening after evening it was like enduring a terrible ordeal, and once it was over there would be others, every day, for all the days to come. She would become accustomed to it, that much was certain, and in some way her mental strength would get the better of Squinter's physical strength. Dora Pagani's husband, for example, had ended his days on top of his wife, one evening when his heart gave out. Sooner or later something in Squinter would go too – he wasn't as young as he had been, and rural men are broken sooner than others – and then she would harness the little advantage she had to put things back in place, and before she did anything else she would go and sleep in another room.

She decided that from that moment onwards she would do nothing but wait, gradually trying to plumb his weakness. In the meantime, she would get used to him as one gets used to a lingering cough or a persistent sore. She was proud of this conclusion and the plan filled her with a strange and intense self-respect. That also involved paying a certain attention to her surroundings, beginning with the house where she still lived. First of all she scraped the black from the copper pots hanging on the walls, then she moved on to the larder, which she cleared of its cobwebs and the dead flies that had been lying there for God knows how long. Since Squinter never came home before half-past five in the evening, she developed the habit of going to the vegetable garden to pick vegetables and make herself some soup before he came back. She hoped that her absence from the table would trouble him and make him think. But among all the thoughts that Squinter had this was not one of them, given that he had not taken a woman into his house in order to have thoughts. Libera tried, then she gave up and started waiting for him again so that they could have dinner together, which allowed her to study him, observe the changes in his face in the direction she hoped, to find in the maze of his wrinkles the next step towards her goal.

Squinter's silent imperturbability was not designed to please her. He sat motionless where he was and gazed straight into his bowl, calmly, as calmly as anything, as if he had time, all the time in the world. And in fact he did have time, he was aware of having lots of time, which meant that she was the one who emerged pale and weary from her thoughts.

Exactly two months after the wedding something unexpected happened, something she had not predicted but which didn't trouble her because she would be able to use it to her own advantage. She thought she would have to tell Squinter straight away, that very evening, but to do so she would have to talk to him. Thinking about it, they had never talked to one another. She would speak to him this evening. She would address a word to him, one word, just once; if he replied, then those words might multiply to two or three; over the evenings that followed they might exchange some impressions about the harvest, just to speak, to loosen their tongues. And then perhaps he would ask her about saucepans, laundry or sewing, and then one word would draw out another and the word would be full of yearning for lost things.

'I need to tell you something, Michelangelo,' she said to him that evening when they were sitting at the table, and she studied that stubborn, unsmiling face.

As if struck by a noise in the distance, Squinter stirred slightly, because since the day of their marriage he hadn't heard Libera utter his name, and couldn't in fact remember ever having been called Michelangelo; then he lowered his head towards his plate.

'I need to tell you something,' she said again in a louder voice.

'Speak, Liberatina,' he said in a clear voice, to give her the pleasure of hearing the sound of her name.

'Oh, that!' she exclaimed, startled. 'One: my name is not Liberatina, but Libera. Two: I need to give you a piece of information that concerns us both, and I would be grateful for a crumb of attention,' she said, irritated by the confidence with which Squinter had addressed her for once, because what happened in bed was one thing, and quite another this unwarranted overfamiliarity, spoiling the name that she cherished above all else.

'Fine, Libera,' Squinter replied, wounded by the violence with which she had reclaimed her name. 'What do you need to tell me?'

'I'm pregnant, Michelangelo...' she said in a single breath, as if fearing that the words might dry up in her throat. 'Did you understand what I said?'

A faint light slipped across Squinter's wooden face, like the pale reflection of an emotion. Alert to the moment, Libera decided to take advantage of it.

'It means that we will be sleeping in different rooms, but I would be grateful to you if you could be so kind as to let me have your room and go and sleep somewhere else.'

'Go on,' he said, bringing his eyes back to his bowl to conceal a slight blush.

'I've finished.'

'Is that all?' he asked, bringing to his mouth the big handkerchief that he wore between his neck and his shirt collar in the field to dry his sweat.

'That's all.'

'Best of luck,' he said, and picked up his full glass from the table.

'The child will grow according to my rules, and study. I don't want it touching the soil with so much as a foot.'

'Fine.'

'And when it's big enough it will leave this place, it will take to the seas. It will discover new worlds and speak other languages.'

'If you want, yes.'

'So tell me, will you leave me your room?' she asked again, giving him a sideways look.

Squinter didn't answer that question, and when Libera repeated it in a louder voice, striking the table with her fists, he got up and walked to the bedroom.

And with that all Libera's private confidence collapsed, leaving her to muse on her condition, legs heavy, eyes downcast. The longer she sat there without moving, the more she felt that she was reflecting deeply on what was happening, when in fact she wasn't thinking about anything apart from the only idea that came to her aid: she had to wait, just wait for something to come along and liberate the help required to change the situation. If only she could at least have found some pleasure in it, as he did when he lay on top of her.

The fact was that, things had changed. One fine day she had woken up in a life that was hers and not hers, and with abhorrent dependability the day rose and faded only to remind her of it.

She rose to her feet and went to the window. It was almost February, and the fields were covered with frost, the air was thick with it. A night bird, fallen from a tree, rolled over on the ground, then whirled off without a cry.

Libera half-closed her eyes as a single thought entered her mind, and said to herself: 'He will have to die on me sooner or later.' Then she got her breath back and opened her eyes wide in bewilderment. 'He will have to die on me sooner or later.'

Estella

This was how things should have gone, although I have no way of confirming it: one fine day, when Libera's husband and son were brought to her laid out on two wooden planks, the husband and son she had been stubbornly convinced she didn't love and had had serious words with herself to persuade herself of the fact: one day when she had reached the lowest rung of her despair, her eyes clouded and her hair stalks of stubble; from that day Libera, who had talked to me a lot, especially when the winds rose, and asked me questions for which I had no answer, didn't come back, and stopped asking those questions.

I waited for weeks for her return, and then one night I dreamt of the Angel's Grotto, that death-hungry portal, and I dreamt of a woman's face like a dried-up plant, a woman in exile spinning around in circles. She must have fallen down that hole, I thought when I woke up, through inattention, or perhaps she hurled herself down it, or she waited for a gust of wind to send her in. By then she was so gaunt, so thin, that the merest puff of wind could have carried her off.

The years have passed, but I think of her often. Now that I could attempt an answer to her questions – even a dishonest answer, what does it matter? Now that I would be quite grateful for the effort, here of all places, in this beggarly village, stripped of everything, there is no grace for me and I am left clinging to its walls. I look at the houses, now that they're all the same, with no names carved on their facades: they are the colour of fresh-dug soil; they have ferns, nettles, moss growing all over them; they have cracks that are ultimately comforting. Perhaps they will fall down one day, but for now they are still standing.

I will have to tell Libera that if she returns to the house on the twisted alleyway, or to Squinter's house – the house that fell in on her, that house in which the smoke from the stove stung her eyes on evenings when the north wind blew, or the warm wind from the mountains – she will find them appeased, she will find her father and husband and her son, cradled by the night, relieved at last because there is no longer any cause for suffering. Fates have been levelled by abandonment, and every house – every house is now a theatre, with the wings in disarray, the stage creaking underfoot, a theatre in which anyone can appear, even those who have never before set foot on such boards. Every evening, at some undecided hour, they can regroup here, with a great rustling of garments, as if they were washed-up actors, mimes, extras, all rejected long ago and all of them failures. Beneath the uneasy, flashing light, eventually a space will be created in which the new expectations will arise, and even those who have always been left behind will breathlessly arrive at last.

Had the village gone on living, it would be known that in one of the mountain caves there is a hole that hides a multitude of frozen bones: the remains of those who died of the plague in 1656 and who, at some point, had moved away from the village and sought refuge in the Angel's Grotto. Here, sitting on the edges of the trench carved out by moisture, they prepared for the moment to come: when the weight of their own dead bodies would drag them down to join the others below. Sometimes it would happen that a little girl did not fall ill, despite being in continuous contact

with the lesions of the others, especially her mother's.
Too young to have a grasp of death, she imagined that the
piled-up bodies in the hole were men and women who had
fallen asleep. Then, when her mother too slipped into the
trench, she thought she had fallen asleep and waited for her
to awaken.

Many others threw themselves into that hole. They
went there on purpose, because you didn't just end up there
by chance, you had to make an effort to go there, among the
rocks that rise from slope to slope; behind you are the ribs
of the valleys and the distant range of the Gelbison, the
holy mountain; ahead of you only the ridges of the Alburno.
When you reach the middle of the plain, where the ascent
to the cave begins, the ground is a mass of pointed things,
as if from there onwards the vegetation had stopped
growing; up there the light has a frozen colour that looks
like no other, the trees don't move, the clouds don't drift.

Giacinto

The purpose of another cave, dear to the people of Alento and called the Cave of the Landslide, was very different: in summertime this was where the eponymous statue of the Madonna was stored. The cave was dug into a slope of the Alburno, not deep but quite wide, and on the first Sunday in May it was the destination of a propitiatory procession for a good crop, from the church to the mouth of the cave – a procession that was repeated in autumn, but this time to keep the land solid when the rains came.

In the May procession the statue was carried on the backs of big men, accompanied by the faithful who walked along the road to a point above the cave, to question the statue about water and the crop and in some way apply pressure to its decisions.

Other parish statues were also carried in procession, because it was the fitting thing to do. The task of establishing the respective ranks of the saints, encouraging agreement among the faithful, who were also ready to fight for the sequence of the statues, fell to Giacinto the town crier, who saw himself first and foremost as a guard, given his past as a former light cavalryman in Pinerolo. And indeed, having difficulty adapting to the harsh local dialect, he preferred to retain his Piedmontese accent while he still had the memory of its intonation.

It was from the churchyard that Giacinto drew up the formations with a wave of his whip. He had abandoned the habit of lance and shield in favour of a bamboo riding crop, but as he directed the pace to the bearers of the saints he now adopted a liturgical cadence. He called the statues by name: 'Come on, then, Mary! The Madonna is a woman and

I put her first, even before the Almighty,' and as the statue passed he gave a chivalrous bow.

Then, with a sharp northern accent, he said: 'Come on, then, George,' acknowledging the saint's priority, perhaps because of his knight's helmet, lance and shield.

'Come on, then, Anthony,' and with a kindly smile he greeted the passage of the humble saint with his boyish face.

And last of all: 'Come on, then, Vito! Come on, come on, come on!' and the tone became almost paternal, as if to comfort the saint for being the last and the most unassuming.

For the rest of the year, Giacinto lent his voice to the village as town crier, even though he wasn't the official town crier, which meant that he had neither uniform nor salary, unlike the street-sweeper or the keeper of the cemetery. Still, the authorities had promised that sooner or later they would deliberate on his official appointment because he was a good worker and deserved a hat and a wage. Until then he would have to settle for the handful of coins that they were able to give him. Giacinto settled for this for a few years, during which time he never neglected to deliver his announcements. And he waited for so long that his announcements changed from the cry 'On the orders of the *signor podestà* ...' to: 'The mayor wishes it to be known ...'.

The most important announcements were institutional, and Giacinto delivered them over several consecutive evenings at dusk, when people were already gathered at home. Let's imagine it was time to go and look at the tax statements at the village hall: Giacinto announced them three in a row, and the people of Alento, hearing shouted words about taxes, darkened and said to him, 'May your voice die in your throat,' as if he were personally responsible for the levies taken.

It was his task to inform the villagers of the start of the school year, and of the period during which animals could be taken to pastures as permitted by civic use. His was the voice that announced the movements of the landslide and, in the same town, the arrival in the village of merchants with whom it was hoped that good deals could be made. Every now and again he announced the organisation of pilgrimages to the nearby sanctuaries or to the temple of the blessed Gionni, erected by popular subscription.

For thirty years Giacinto issued his daily proclamations, without the use of a trumpet or megaphone or wine-funnel to amplify his voice, while walking around the streets of the village, breathless because he could see nothing but shadows. Before he went to bed he treated his dry throat with an infusion of rue, saying to himself: 'I will be a guard. I will be more than a guard. What will the street-sweeper say when he sees me with a liveried hat? And what will Peppino the undertaker say?'

Except that the hat never came.

'The factory hasn't sent it,' the council usher said, 'but it will come, you can be sure of that.'

'Can't anything be done to speed it up?' he asked disappointedly every time. 'I'm getting old, and I still haven't seen it.'

'There's nothing we can do: the factory is in Naples, there's a whole sea in between and it takes time for it to get here. But you'll see.'

So it was that Giacinto came to imagine that only a holy hand could speed up the practice. He could try and put himself under the protection of a politician, a Christian Democrat, for example, because in southern Italy the Christian Democrats were the most powerful and would have no problem intervening on his behalf, even if there was a sea in between. But on the other hand, what did he have to offer, poor, alone in the world and half-blind as he was? Not even his vote, since in June 1946 he had publicly declared that he would never again vote for the great disappointment that followed on from the electoral result. The king, only the king, could have looked after poor people like himself, but the Communists had put an end to that and what good had it done him? They were poor as church mice at the start and poor as church mice at the end as well, but now without the paternal figure of the king.

He had no option but to seek the holy hand elsewhere, beating a startling path of the kind open to people like himself. It was the path of devotion, holy fire like the honey mixed with walnuts that Giacinto tasted only once a year, at Christmas. In other people's eyes the business with the hat would not have seemed to call for a recourse to the divine, but in his own, which could see nothing else, it was his very reason for staying alive. The divine, which had an indisputable authority over others and exercised it capriciously, had a moderate influence on his existence. Besides, what did he have to lose? With or without the divine, he got on with his life, which was not much lovelier than that of a dazed rat that anyone could have finished off as they saw fit. So he would try the path of devotion for the hat – let the others eat him alive! – but if his prayer went unanswered he would not try again, that much was certain, because he wasn't keen on swindlers, not even if they went by the name of God.

Where that was concerned, he knew that recently

groups of devotees of the Blessed Gionni had left Alento, and along with thousands of others coming from outside they filled a kind of sanctuary set up in great haste in Serconia. Giacinto was aware of it because he himself had announced the trips.

No one knew for certain whether the blessed one was really due for sanctification: the family said so, and that was enough. Underlying it all was the story of Gionni, who had died after being run over by a lorry driven by his uncle. The boy's father, mad with rage, decided to take his revenge on the brother who had killed his son, but the family tragedy was averted by Nenè, the sister of the pair, who declared out of the blue that she had been filled with her nephew's spirit. The rancour immediately subsided, and from that day Gionni's soul entered his aunt's body on a daily basis. She began to speak to the curious who crowded to see her, and she also began to utter curses, to formulate prophesies, to promise cures in Gionni's name, with the result that the curious were joined by the disabled, the blind and the paralysed.

Soon the doctors found themselves without patients because the ailing hurried to Serconia, especially since the bishop had forbidden Nenè and her followers from entering the church. To cope with the mass of people who asked her for an audience every day, Nenè was forced to distribute numbered tickets to give everyone orderly access to her presence. Because there wasn't enough room, however, she had to enlarge the house. Major developments, in short.

When Giacinto set foot in the holy place he bought a figure of the saint, a key ring and a knick-knack bearing a picture of the Blessed Gionni. He could only make out the outlines of the objects, but he had been advised to present himself before the priestess with the relics that he had already bought, and that was what he did. Out of caution he also bought a record of the sermons of Nenè that he would have been able to listen to comfortably at home on his record player, if he had had a record player.

He had been told that Nenè, who was about fifty years old, was something to see: fat and florid, she closed her eyes and all at once became pale and small. The crowd immediately pressed around her and waited for the fit to pass, while she shuddered from head to toe and chewed on her fingers; then with a jolt she came to, but said she was no longer herself, she said she was Gionni and started speaking and responding to the invocations of the faithful. Then she withdrew into a kind of hut and received anyone who had a favour to ask of her, not more than fifty or sixty cases a day. She didn't ask for money, but everyone left an offering.

Giacinto was received after a wait of about three hours. The hut was stuffy, with a smell of vinegar and possibly of stale urine. Seeing him come forward, stumbling and leaning on a stick, Nenè pre-empted him: 'Can't you see?'

'Not really. I see only shadows,' he replied, as if alarmed by the insight hurled out of the blue between him and the divine. This woman knew everyone's stories, he thought, his own included, so in all probability she already knew about the hat.

'I imagine you're here for your eyesight.'

Giacinto hesitated for a moment, then thought about the journey he had taken to get there, about the money he had spent on relics, of the offering that he would have to leave before going: if he managed to receive two things at once, so much the better.

'If you can, why not,' he said to her contentedly.

'Let me put my hand on your head. Come closer.'

The man came closer and, closing his eyes, allowed the priestess's fat hands to touch his temples. He heard her grunting as if she were in pain, then she began screaming as if she were being murdered: 'Eyes return, return, O eyes.' Giacinto slowly opened his eyelids and glanced around: the shadows dividing him from the divine presence had not dispersed. He deduced from this that nothing had changed, and his eyes had not returned. With a heavy heart he closed them again, and he was struck not by what he could see but by what he could hear. The priestess had begun to spit on the ground like a sheep afflicted with catarrh. He turned slowly to the side to examine the watery lumps, but at that moment he felt an insistent itch behind his ear and, lifting his stick slightly, he scratched himself.

'What are you doing?' the woman asked him, clearly annoyed.

'I'm sorry, I felt an itch back there and couldn't help myself.'

'What exactly did you come here for? Don't you care about your eyesight? You seem like a halfwit.'

'I really came here about the hat. If we were to extend the request somewhat, we could include the eyesight. But primarily I want the hat.'

'The hat?'

'That's right, the braided hat that's supposed to be coming from the factory but never arrives. Didn't you know that?'

'What do you want from me? Go away this instant.'

'Isn't the hat a favour like the others? I bought all these trinkets on purpose, look,' and he took from his pockets the votive objects that he had bought and, unaware of what he was doing, dropped them one by one on the seated priestess's head.

'Go away, I said.'

'I also bought the record with your voice on it; tomorrow I will also buy a record player so that I can hear you. Can't the blessed one go in a dream to the people at the factory in Naples to tell them to bring the hat to Giacinto of Alento, because Giacinto needs it?'

'Out! Out of my house.'

Giacinto paused for a moment; then, when the woman began to groan like a bird with a broken wing, he stepped aside and moved slowly towards the exit, making his way through two rows of the faithful, who shoved and insulted him. Everyone was talking, and no one had a kind word for him. No one had told him it might end like this. A strange day, a really strange day in which he had begun the approach to the divine and it had ended immediately. 'Gionni, pray for us,' cried the two old women blocking the exit from the holy place with their bodies. 'Gionni, bestow your favours upon us!'

No, he hadn't believed it. Deep down he hadn't believed it.

Outside, he began to count the footsteps separating him from the coach that would take him back to the village, with the other people from the village who were still waiting near the priestess. When he was halfway there, he heard quick and heavy footsteps coming up threateningly behind him, and then a very high-pitched cry of 'Bastard!' Then he felt a dull blow on the back of his neck. Then nothing. Then more nothing. That was what they had given him. With the report of a gunshot, although no gun was present, a single blow to the head knocked him to the ground, and there he stayed.

Two villagers came and picked him up about an hour later. He wasn't dead, at least he didn't seem to be, but they couldn't wake him. They hoisted him up and put him on a sofa, but no one thought to take him to the nearest hospital, not out of meanness, not that, but such an obvious thought didn't occur to anyone, since they were all still under the spell of the priestess.

That evening, in the village, Giacinto's voice wasn't heard at the usual hour of his announcements.

'Is he dead?' everyone wondered.

'Not yet.'

'Did he pass out?'

'No, he fell on his face. He was brought home drenched in blood.'

Giacinto wailed all night, and every now and again he moved his head, turning it to face the window. From there he imagined he could see the whole of the Gulf of Salerno enclosed in the crescent of the Gulf of Naples. Naples, Naples, Naples.

The factory was in Naples, and that was where his hat was. But for the sea in between, he could have walked all the way to what was rightfully his. The doctor who tended to him raised his hands and ordered someone to go to the rectory, to Don Basilio, for extreme unction. Giacinto clung on until dawn, then passed away.

The funeral was held on Sunday. The local authorities were there, and the carabinieri, and there were flowers everywhere. Don Basilio delivered the speech usually given on grand occasions. It was a lovely funeral – presentiments of eternity mingled with the flowers. Lying on the casket was a hat with beautiful gold braid on the front, and every-one noticed how the yellow of the braid matched the colour of the pine coffin.

Estella

I would like to tell Marcello that, having reached this point in our long life, I would happily hang on to his arm, I would cling to it for the last stretch.

I know I have dug myself dungeons of loneliness, but how I hated the clang of the metal door that I closed myself, with several turns of the key. I want to tell him I was so convinced that I couldn't be loved that loving me must have been difficult.

The day he left, he closed his eyes to bring his face close to mine in one last painful farewell, as if we were parting for ever; obviously I pushed him away, as I always did with approaches of this kind. Then that smile, so bright and alive, that mocking smile as he grew up, that smile that I had seen so often distorting his mouth, accompanied the usual words of contempt and the satisfaction of leaving me to rot here. He actually said 'rot'. But what could I do if the dull indolence of the senses kept me far from any contact that wasn't pious or actually charitable?

When he left – and with him, one after the other, the rest of the village's inhabitants – I tried to ignore the fact that only my body and his existed. I took refuge in a pit of centuries and roots, I let the seasons flow past me, not moving a finger, not wanting to know anything more. I became nothing but a defrocked nun, caught in the whirlpool of an ineptitude that was all my own; the cloistered whiteness of my face reveals it, even though I left the cloister a long time ago. A heart of thorns that ran to climb the trees, particularly the elm, hair unkempt, feet bare and dirty, and from there, from that makeshift pulpit, intoned chants to the wind, to the rivers, to the earth, with the air of a madwoman.

And also I expected something. I hoped to emerge from it intact. In fact, I emerged from it lacerated and even more dispossessed than before. Now I look at my marked skin, that skin so weak because it has no memory of embraces, and I can't bear it.

I should have thought of it before. It's fine, it's fine, I should have done. But while he was here, Marcello became a habit for me, and his attempts to kiss me nothing but a mute breath.

He knew and forgave me, although by that time I was no longer to blame. He had given me what he was able to give me. But what did I know? Only that it's difficult to return love when you have never had any; it's a hard thing to recognise it if one has never had a way of knowing it. This does not excuse me, in fact it oppresses and torments me. I could have given him the same love, the same tenderness, in the same way that he gave them to me, learning from his awkward gestures how he offered them to me, day after day, unaware of the significance that they assumed as soon as they left his body. Still, when I was about to yield them to him, he appeared to my inflexible eyes like one blessed by fate, on which I would not have hung the burden of my sorrows. Marcello, deep down, had survived. He had had a house, a father, a loving mother, and what had I had? None of the good things that come from such things. Over the years that have passed as they must, I feel as if I have had only a single thought. I was deceived by love – the love of someone who holds out a hand to you, a hand concealing some gorgeous treat, who wipes the blood from your knees when you fall. And I didn't want to feel that anymore, I didn't want to feel unloved. No one should be condemned to see the contempt in the eyes of the one who brought you into the world, to be born, to reach a certain point and a little further than that: all denied. Denied the healing word – *take care of me because I can't make it on my own*. Denied the chance to reach the source of all beauty. The love that moves the world. While I was moved only by the abyss within.

Besides, what had the cloister been if not another attempt to find a place to be? A place that was also mine, just a bit, would have been enough for me. Then when I failed that test too, I returned to the mountains, I returned to the peaks where sky touched rock, hoping for a homecoming, a return to the cold, which has its blessings. To small things with well-defined outlines. To the graves shaken by their old inhabitants. Here, between mountain and mountain, I tried to reassemble the pieces, because there are different ways of saving yourself. I have always doubted the idea of perpetual salvation, in fact I never believed in it. Provisional salvation – the typical salvation of those who make it out, the frail salvation of the survivors – I feel that it can belong to me, like the abandoned houses all around that seem to be collapsing on top of me, all battered, all broken: they resemble my wounds, this network of cracks. Perhaps I should be worried, I see the wounds erupting, more frightening still than the cracks in the houses that I have around me. And in fact I don't, I draw strength from them, I have put gaps in them to let in air and light. They are something. They are mine. Like a possibility. And look, Marcello: they hold.

Lucia Parisi

There was a flash, and electric light arrived in the Parisi household one November evening in 1960.

It had reached the village forty years before, and among the natives there was no one who didn't remember the evening of 28 July 1923 when the electrical substation was welcomed by a cortege behind a marching band and, immediately afterwards, blessed by the parish priest, with the mayor supporting the train of his stole.

That wasn't how things went in the surrounding countryside, where there were so few private connections that they could be counted on the fingers of one hand. On the main roads, however, the webs of wires almost entirely replaced the paraffin lamps, which now hung lifeless in the air, bathed in loneliness.

Consiglio Parisi decided that electric light had to come inside the house because modernity was knocking at the door, and it had to be welcomed in. And on the basis of nothing ventured nothing gained, for four months on the trot he went into the village, all the way to the council offices, to ask for a connection, a connection that was the first in the whole district of Terzo di Mezzo.

Custoda, unlike her husband, was in no great hurry for modernity, since she had never wanted for light in the house, had never lacked it thanks to the paraffin lamps which brought bright daylight to the darkness. She had also tried to oppose the project – standing motionless for hours in front of the brass lamp, with its huge glass chimney – but to no avail, eventually dropping the idea and retreating to her corner by the fire. Besides, as she very well knew, some battles aren't worth fighting.

Their three children each responded to the new arrival according to how useful it was to them. The two boys were pleased by the idea of no longer studying by the feeble light of the little lamps, while Lucia didn't know how to respond to a profusion of light in the home, given that she didn't have to study because her father had only sent her to school up to a certain point.

The connection man turned up at the door towards the end of November, wearing an oversized overall of an intricate blue that the children marvelled at. Even Custoda couldn't help staring at his outfit, before irritably looking away because she was concerned about the devil's handiwork which the man had come to bring into her house and of which, she was certain, no good would come.

The connection man hastily greeted Consiglio, who welcomed him as one welcomes those who free us from darkness, and set about his task with great resolution.

When the time came, the men of the house gathered around the dinner table and waited in silence for the flash of light to come. It was a triumph.

Lucia, like her mother, was immediately suspicious of those metal wires, and, even though she couldn't help opening her eyes wide in the face of such brilliance, she retreated to a corner, disdaining the man who had come all the way out to establish the connection. Given that her eyes were filled with large tears from staring continuously at the bright lamp, her distrust increased, and along with it a premonition of worse to come.

But it was on the day of the autumn festival – a few days after the connection was made – that she became convinced once and for all that the electric light was a great swindle, a trap and nothing more.

That morning, well before dawn, she had taken the goats to the pasture, and in spite of the intense cold, which had made the animals' eyes bulge, she had left them grazing and returned to the farm before the strike of ten. She still had two or three things to do before she could go up to the village for the propitiatory procession, and she had to get a move on because Tonino di Vitantonio would wait for her in the square for no more than ten minutes, since his was the right shoulder that would carry the Madonna of the Landslide, a privilege granted by preference to the men who had come back to the village from the war or, for want of a war, those who had returned from military service.

But today was the day on which the devil himself had decided to put a spanner in the works, making appropriate use of the very thing that Custoda held in such contempt. What else, in fact, could he have acted through if not via that useless electric light that had entered their house via the front door and taken root in everyone's head as if it were in charge? And whose fault could it be if not the devil's, if Lucia, having returned breathless from the pasture, had lifted the handle of the broom too high while sweeping the floor, striking the lamp, which, the very height of treachery, had shattered into a thousand tiny pieces?

Lucia knew that Consiglio would not tolerate such lapses of attention in his house, and more particularly he would not permit them on her part, given that she already had the gall to have been born a girl when in every respectable household the first-born had always been male. Now her lack of attention had irremediably compromised Consiglio's dream of modernity; for three days he had contemplated the lamp with satisfaction, as if haloed in the new wealth, which did not refer to any other underlying wealth and which he therefore valued as wealth in itself.

Even before her father found out, Lucia felt a kind of exhaustion falling upon her; this was not a new sensation to her, because Consiglio was forever telling her off about something, but this time it was serious.

Huddled in a corner by the fire, Custoda watched her daughter trying in vain to catch her breath as she picked up the fragments of shattered glass and put them in her lap. A gurgle in her stomach revealed to her the fear that already assailed her. Looking up, she could in fact see her husband advancing across the room, his face a tangle of veins, showing genuine fury. In an instant the man was behind his daughter, and without a word he began beating her with all the strength that a father like himself could show, particularly on such occasions.

Lucia, bent double like a bag of turnips, prepared to receive the blows without attempting to defend herself, only counting the moments of respite granted to her between one blow and the next.

Then noises started coming from a distance, and that was enough to make Consiglio stop and raise his head towards the window to see if someone was coming. Since no one was, he returned his attention to that lump of flesh and uselessness that was his daughter. He was not yet mollified but already a bit more hesitant.

It was at that moment that Lucia thought of pretending to die, which would certainly have placated her father because no one touches the dead, particularly the dead in poor people's houses. So she fell to the ground and froze. In her rage, she took advantage of the moment to imagine Tonono di Vitantonio standing impatiently in the square, an image rendered even more cruel by the silhouette of her ruthless father. From behind her eyelids, in fact, she was aware of the arms still tensed and the face motionless and terrible, nostrils dilated as if on the point of sneezing.

She refused to admit to herself that Tonino di Vitantonio wouldn't come looking for her if she didn't get there in time. They hadn't seen each other since he had left for military service, and in the only card he had sent her before coming home he specified this day and this time, asking her not to be late.

Gripped by boundless self-pity, she thought of the last thing that remained to be done, after which she would be able to die there on the floor. She convinced herself that there was no other option, and, regardless of what this desperate enterprise might cost her, she let out a groan into which she seemed to entrust all the life remaining within her.

'Father,' she said, 'please forgive me for the act of inattention which, a short time ago, destroyed the lamp and the light of this house. I beg you, but I know it's not enough. Please grant me permission to go into the village for the procession and ask the Lord himself forgiveness for my sin of stupidity. Allow me, father, to do that for my soul.'

As soon as the last word left her lips, Lucia covered her eyes with her hand, as if fearing that her father's feet might strike her head.

There were a few moments of respite, during which it was all Custoda could do not to fall from her chair, moved to the brink of tears by her daughter's unexpected display of spirit. Then she broke the silence with a sharp series of coughs directed at her husband.

Consiglio, still frozen in his serious pose, felt something like a breath dispersing his rage to the wind. How could he resist such a request for forgiveness? His daughter had spoken of *soul*, and who was he to deny her comfort? Only the Almighty could deny it to her, not he, who could decide on the wellbeing of his children up to a certain point. Besides, he had always treated them with kindness, and the blows delivered by his hands were meant to correct, never to offend, because offence is for cowards.

At that moment he looked at his daughter, and he looked at her with something like a mother's sympathy, almost aware that he loved her. She had spoken of *soul*, after all, and who was he to refuse her? Thus it was that he nodded kindly to her request, accompanying his agreement with a broad gesture of blessing that meant 'Arise and go'.

Lucia, recovering instantly, grabbed and kissed the hand that had struck her only a moment before, almost dazed by the success of her ploy. She looked for a moment at Custoda, who had already stopped looking at her, and immediately afterwards, her head still crawling with the blows she had received, ran to the well to wash. An old mirror hanging just above the washbasin returned a yellowed image filled with ugliness: face swollen, eyes ringed and, a little lower down, the red print of her father's fingers. The sight dispirited her still further and she furiously pulled herself away from the mirror because she certainly didn't have time to deal with her wretched life right now.

She ran home and hurried to change, putting on the dress that she had stitched herself – well made, yes, but without the slightest extravagance. She looked at herself in the mirror again and all in all she found herself acceptable. She ran outside again, paying attention to the two or three damp spots that always formed in the gravel, and dragged the mule from the stable, weary and ancient but still capable of climbing the road up to the village. She sat herself on its rump, and immediately the old mule's panting harmonised with Lucia's sighs and heartbeats. The autumn wind and rain no longer seemed to torment the resting countryside and instead were caressing it, so much so that the fallen leaves seemed to revive in a yearning tremble, and look: even the trees didn't look like scrawny bones any more but appeared to be filling with fresh sap.

Almost without noticing, Lucia found herself in the village, and with one final effort on the mule's part she reached the square, where the saints – judging by the clusters of waiting people – had not yet appeared. Looking more than ever like a proud peacock, with wind-ruffled plumage and coated with a dust that looked like the dust of neglect, Lucia looked around in search of Tonino di Vitantonio and saw him half-submerged between two rows of the faithful.

When she made to approach him, tugging on the reins of the mule that now refused to move and was therefore braying its head off, Tonino gestured to her to stop. He came towards her, and did so hesitantly, as if with each step he were about to turn back. As soon as he was near her, he muttered some words that Lucia couldn't make out because a festive chime of bells announced the emergence of the saints from the church. Then they both stood aside to allow more people to join in the procession.

He must have had a different view of things, because in the harsh light Lucia struck him as ugly, her face autumnal; she also smelled of mule. He looked around in search of other women's faces, diaphanous and scented with lavender, like the ones he had met in the north and who now, in the village, he could imagine only in his dreams.

'I've got to go, Lucia. I'm carrying the Madonna on my shoulder today,' he said in a mannered voice, staring at a point in the distance.

'Will we see each other again?' she asked.

'I don't know. I don't think so. Better not,' he replied, and walked off with a shrug.

The susurration of those words grew around Lucia, barely reaching her ears. Thin, almost like a whistle, the words made an incomprehensible sound, with no colour but the colour of air, no shape if not the precise shape of a farewell.

She remembered a goat that had expired with its head in the straw; the sound of the breath that issued from it just before it died was like her breathing now, a terrible, sepulchral breath. She looked down at herself and saw that she was crumpled from the journey on the mule, her arms and hands filthy with dust. She had waited for an eternity that day. She had stitched her dress at night by the light of the paraffin lamp. She had wanted it to be blue like the blue of the sea on postcards, a sea that belonged to other people and which she had never seen.

It was then that she made her mind up, because she felt that this was the moment, and because she had made her decision, no catechismal intimations could dissuade her as they had on other occasions in the past. Having had her fill of disappointment, more than was fair, to tell the truth, she no longer wanted to see hands pointing to the place where she was born; she no longer wanted to arrange her features into an expression of patient resignation.

Besides, what was she leaving behind? A smell of the world, sniffed secretly. Exactly as happened with chocolate, the gorgeous treat that her father shared only among his sons, who studied and grew visibly taller by the month, as he would proudly announce. She, admittedly, had plenty of raisins and currants, and Custoda said it was better to take what you have and be thankful. Except that now her feelings merged into a single impulse, and she no longer had any wish for the prudence of her mother, whose words echoed in her head like footsteps climbing stairs of resignation.

She took the mule and walked towards the road leading out of the village, at a quick pace because she didn't want to change her mind. Having reached the highest point on the plateau, where the road seemed to detach itself from the ground and continue on its own suspended in the air, she looked down. There was a deep trench, already iced over, full of dead birds and clumps of withered weeds. The trench was there in front of her, welcoming, waiting. She couldn't think about it for too long, because these things require impulsiveness. And in fact she stopped thinking about it.

What had that metallic light given her? In the dusty haze of the paraffin lamps, everything would still have been possible, everything still to be done. Under the grim glare of the electric light, everything was finished.

Consiglio Parisi

It wasn't the first time that death had entered the home of Consiglio Parisi. It had happened before, in 1957, on a morning drowsy with the last of the October sun. Before then, his house had been spared because they didn't count the stillborn twins years before, since they had been dead when they entered the world, a sign that death had met them outside, not inside the house. But since Custoda had liberated herself of two little corpses at once, Consiglio preferred to keep his distance from her for long enough to have a change of air, two or three days, not more, during which he became accustomed to sleeping in the open, using his full granary as an excuse, because thieving raids were frequent at the time.

Custoda thanked her missing children for keeping him away for so long, finally alone in the kind of vestibule that was their bedroom, full of her husband's annoying little knick-knacks; on those few sheltered evenings, she could be woman and baby, mother and unborn daughter, cheeks washed with tears half-illuminated by the faint glow of the lamp.

On that morning in 1957 everyone was at home, including the two boys, who hadn't yet gone back to school. Consiglio was busy reading the newspaper, as he did every morning: he bought it only once a week and read it over all the mornings that followed, glassy-eyed and entirely absorbed in the marvel of the paper, holding it at arm's length, because there was no shortage of things to read in those word-covered pages. He had inherited from his father the inclination to trust only what came off the printing press; his own name had been taken from the newspaper, because on the day of his birth the front page had carried a story about a *Consiglio di Stato per le terre liberate* – Council of State for the Lands Freed from the Enemy; this had appeared to old Parisi as a sign of great significance. He gave his son the name Consiglio and blessed him.

Custoda, unlike her husband, mistrusted those columns of words like the final spray of a tide that was rising elsewhere. Words that concerned him in some way and which, to boot, were compressed on a great sheet of paper that smelled of shoe polish.

'Custoda, the only reason you have a head is to keep your hair on,' Consiglio said to her irritably every time she mentioned the coins spent on the purchase of the newspaper, comparing the cost with the current price of bread.

On that morning in 1957, Custoda was woken by a noise from the kitchen, a continuous noise like an impatient hand tapping on a pile of papers. She got up to see. Nothing in the kitchen was moving apart from her, looking around at all the sleeping things. The tapping sound came from the fireplace, where some kind of animal must have been trapped. She picked up the poker and knelt down beside the hearth. A bird must have got caught in the last section of the chimney, just before it widened into the stove. She tried to touch it, to make it come out. But the bird went on fluttering from one side to the other, unable to find a way of freeing itself, and, as if crazed with terror at making contact with the iron structure, started uttering cries that Custoda recognised immediately. It was then that she decided to slip her arm into the fireplace, because the creature must on no account fall into the house. She finally brushed its feathers and tried to grab it to push it upwards, but failed because the bird had taken refuge in a crevice. So she picked up the poker again and thought about delivering a firm blow to dislodge it. 'You're an animal,' she said, 'off you fly.' After her first attempt failed she tried a second time, then a third and a fourth. Now in a rage, she couldn't stop because this owl or whatever it was mustn't fall into her house, it mustn't lay eyes on her or her sons, not now that Mariuccia was so weak. She went on thrusting the poker up the chimney without realising that her blows had drowned out the bird's cries, which could now no longer be heard. She thrust the poker up again and then had to stop: the bird fell out, brushing her knees, bloodied and dead.

There was a wide table in the middle of the room and Custoda sat down at it. She held the dead bird in her lap and stared at it as if her own life were entangled in that stiff plumage. It was as if a ruthless hand were twisting and twisting a nail in her head: Mariuccia.

Deep drowsiness weighed down her eyelids; she would have liked to go back to bed and put everything off until tomorrow. But at that moment the door of the room opened and Consiglio appeared.

'Custoda, I'd like to understand what's going through your head. You made such a racket that you woke me up.'

'There was a bird in the chimney. I was trying to free it.'

'I can see how you've freed it!'

'It was a screech owl.'

'It gets worse. Custoda, you're a madwoman and this would have to happen to me. If only I could go back in time. If only I hadn't been in such a hurry to get married!' Consiglio's usual litany had started up again this morning, and this morning, once again, Custoda's voice was trained to reply in a reassuring sing-song, as it had been doing for eighteen years. In fact she said, 'My dowry far exceeded your possessions. That's why you were in a hurry to get married.'

'Listen to her! Your dowry was a piece of wasteland that you had to sell to pay your legal fees.'

'That piece of land brought in forty thousand lira, and I wouldn't have had to pay any legal fees if it hadn't been for that fraud.'

'The law condemned you,' Consiglio reminded her inexorably.

'I never went to Micchetto's land,' Custoda replied imperturbably.

He: 'That's what you say, but Franco Zonzi saw you with the goats down there and referred it to the judge.'

She: 'The testimony was false. Franco Zonzi has never been a good man, you can tell by how he ended up.'

'However he ended up,' Consiglio concluded, 'the law says that on that day, at that time, you were on Micchetto's land; the goats ate the bushes and you paid the damages.'

'And Micchetto shared the money with Franco Zonzi,' Custoda added, but at this point she always felt exhausted, because the sentence had been a blow from which she had never recovered. 'The law believed them and I'm not surprised. But you're my husband, you should have believed in me. It had been months since I had gone to the pasture, we sent Lucia there instead. How could they swear they'd seen me down there?'

'I only believe what the law says, and if the law says you were on Micchetto's land with the goats on those days, then that's where you were.'

'Franco Zonzi was killed in his own house a year ago, suffocated with a piece of fabric.'

'That's a matter that has nothing to do with me, or with you for that matter. The law didn't establish anything, so nothing happened.'

'But he was killed, the law established that. And it's also clear who killed him, even if there's no proof.'

'Custoda, be quiet. Do you want to end up in even more trouble because of your stupidity? There's no proof to accuse anyone, the law says so. Zonzi was killed, yes, but by himself.'

'With a gag in his mouth?'

'Exactly, and let's end the matter there. You claim to know more than the law, but there's nothing higher than the law. And since it's a higher entity, you can't understand it because you are even more subject to it than everyone else.'

There was a silence. Custoda stayed where she was at the table, still with the owl in her lap. She wanted to say that the higher law that had condemned her was an unjust law, lax with the strong and implacable with the weak. Weak she truly was, because she wasn't rich and, what was more, she was a woman, and her husband never neglected to mention the fact, stressing her inferiority. But she wasn't stupid. She wanted to shout that she had been defrauded, and the words would have issued from her very bones, from the veins she felt she had opened. But what would have been the point? She would have gone on living as if in that strange house that she saw in her dreams at night, a house in mourning in which she was the deceased. The best thing to do was to remain silent, as usual. Without noticing, she clenched her fingers around the body of the owl and uttered a groan of sorrow.

Meanwhile, Consiglio had gone outside to the basin to fetch water and wash before reading the newspaper, which he could never do with his head in confusion and sleep in his eyes.

Custoda ordered her thoughts about the fears that were coming back to assail her now, like the owl in the house with the ice in its eyes. The particularly insinuating fear was that something might happen to Mariuccia, and she imagined the days to come with dread. She got up and started lighting the fire. It was still early, and things were still. She listened for distant voices that might come and comfort her; she pricked up her ears and waited, but in vain: nothing came. Worried, she threw the owl's little body into the fire and stood and watched as it burned; for a moment the lingering terror in the animal's wide eyes reflected her own, and then it went up.

Mariuccia was the last one to be born in the house; she was seven years old and the only Parisi to have the fair hair that came from her mother's family. And she was the most graceful of the Parisis, and that too came from her mother, who was slight, even tiny.

Maruccia's birth had been marked by affliction. For starters, she was not born at home like her brothers, or in any sheltered place. She was born by the side of a road, under a sun that barely gave off any warmth.

It happened along the hill that led from Terzo di Mezzo to the village, on an afternoon in which the wind bent the blades of grass like so many penitent souls. When Custoda, now approaching the end of her term, felt a kick in her belly, she didn't stop and went on climbing. The clock chimed three and there was no one to be seen on the road. A little way away from a dilapidated house that stood balanced on the landslide, Custoda couldn't help dropping to her knees, because she felt as if a thousand hands were grabbing at her womb. Had she had the strong blood of youth she would have got back up and continued up to the village, where someone would have helped her. But she couldn't move. She stayed by the roadside and, making a great effort, prepared to wait. Between one kick and the next, the mischief of her memories returned to torture her, using the excuse of the pain in her womb. Only faint sounds reached her from a distance, and they too sounded drowsy. The stillborn twins years before had come out of her womb in the same way, a sign that they had battled death before succumbing to it.

At that moment, an old woman dressed in black came up with a basket on her back. As soon as she was the right distance away, she glanced at the woman curled up on the ground.

'Sore stomach?' the old woman asked, and Custoda moved her coat aside to show her.

The old woman looked at her, then took the basket off her back and took out a big bottle full of water.

'Take a sip of this,' she said, handing her the bottle.

'Bless you, this will send me on my way,' Custoda said, taking the bottle in both hands.

'You speak well, are you a schoolteacher?' the old woman asked as if struck by Custoda's tone, delicate in spite of the pain she was feeling.

'No, I'm not.'

'But you talk like a schoolteacher.'

'My father made me do a bit of school.'

'And do you know how to read?'

'I know how to read.'

'If I help you with your belly, can you read me a letter? I don't know how to read.'

'Yes, of course,' Custoda replied and smiled at the little old woman who looked like a child.

The old woman took back the bottle, shook it and poured it over Custoda, who flinched beneath the flood.

'Don't worry: water calls to water, and your waters haven't appeared yet.'

Custoda looked at her wet clothes, then felt a liquid coming out of her and running down her legs. She knew the moment had come. The old woman gestured to her to take off her coat, and in spite of the dust that had built up in that roadside ditch, in the open air and with her legs apart, Custoda was ashamed. It was cold, even though the sun was keeping the frost away. The old woman laid the coat out like a carpet so that the life that was about to come into the world didn't immediately make contact with dust, and prepared to welcome it.

The baby emerged after a few minutes of exertions, without wails or tremors.

'Why isn't it crying?' Custoda murmured with her last remaining breath.

'She's alive.'

Then the old woman passed a finger over the baby's mouth in order to break the *liatùra* and prevent stammering, and put light pressure on its cheeks to leave dimples; finally she cut the cord with the knife that she used in the fields, and tied the navel with a length of straw that she pulled from her basket.

'She's beautiful. What are you calling her?'

'We haven't decided,' replied Custoda, who was beginning to recover, in spite of the red patches on her cheeks left over from her exertions. 'My husband would have called a boy Palmiro, because it's the name of an important man that he often finds in the newspaper, so he calls him his friend. He isn't interested in girls' names.'

'Then take my name, it's a pretty one.'

'What's your name?'

'Mariuccia.'

'It really is a pretty name. If my husband agrees, that's what we'll call her.'

'Remember that you're about to enter the period of purification: you have to stay at home for forty days, you mustn't even go to church. Eat a broth of chicken and onions, that makes for good milk.'

'Tell me where you live, Mariuccia, so that I can pay you a visit as soon as I can.'

'My house is only a room, it isn't a house. Don't put yourself to any trouble.'

'But how can I thank you for what you've done?'

'The letter, you have to read me the letter.'

'Do you have it with you?'

'I do, signora, I always carry it with me, it's from Michelino, my son who left for Venezuela.'

'But he knows that you can't read?'

'No. I was ashamed and never told him. He went to school, he had friends in the gentry, and he told them his mother was dead and I was his wet-nurse.'

'And you didn't say anything?'

'No, nothing.'

'You don't have any other children?'

'No, signora. After Michelino was born they gave me the operation.'

Custoda looked at the old woman speaking to her with her head to one side as if to conceal a grimace of pain, but her eyes were still visible, cloudy in their sockets.

The newborn daughter had immediately fallen asleep on her breast. She was a tiny creature, already exhausted, but she had the colours of the sun mixed with the black of the dusty coat in which she was wrapped like a bundle.

'Show me the letter.'

As if she hadn't expected anything else, the old woman went over to the basket, lifting the dry wooden logs that she had carefully stacked in it, and pulled out the cloth in which the letter was wrapped. She laid the package momentarily on the palm of one hand, while with the other she lifted the flaps, with the slow movements of a priest depositing the humeral veil at the end of the rites. Then, holding it tightly between two fingers, she handed Custoda the letter.

Custoda took it. The piece of paper, she reflected, was that woman's reason for living, the source of her reasoning, the most natural thing that could be done, the reasoning of a mother who loves her son. First she scanned the lines without reading them. There weren't many, about ten in all; then she began to read them from the end, because if there were words of affection in the conclusion, there were also sure to be some in the middle. She read and gulped. The letter closed with *Expect no more news from me, because you don't know how to read anyway. Goodbye.*

She read the rest with mounting anxiety and there was nothing there but a definitive farewell to his mother's poverty and ignorance, as if bidding farewell to a prejudice that had followed him through his life.

Meanwhile the old woman kept her eye fixed on the woman's face, to guess from the tiniest movements of her eyes everything that had been kept from her until that moment.

Embarrassed, Custoda made a gesture as if to say, 'Good news.'

'What does he say? Is he well?'

'Don't worry, Mariuccia. Your son is well and has found a good job in Caracas. He is doing well. He says it was good luck for him to leave our poor country. There are more possibilities beyond the sea.'

'And he's not coming back?'

'Not for now. He needs to establish himself. It's better if he stays where he is now.'

'And me, does he ask about me?'

'He certainly does. He hopes you're well and says he won't be able to write often because sending a letter from the other side of the sea is very expensive, and in fact letters that have to cross the sea hardly ever arrive. But he's thinking of you and he loves you very much.'

'That letter arrived two months ago but I was ashamed to ask anyone to read it to me.'

'Is your son very dear to you, Mariuccia?'

'He is everything to me, everything. But now you have to get up, very slowly now, because this is a beautiful day: the day when your daughter was born and I learned that my son hasn't forgotten me.'

On that morning in 1957, Mariuccia woke up looking pale. She made her way slowly into the kitchen, and for a moment Custoda felt superstitious at the sight of her. Then she turned to look at her husband to ask him if he saw much more than a ghost. There was no point because Consiglio was miles away; as always his eyes were fixed on the newspaper, from which nothing could distract him.

Mariuccia wasn't complaining; only the hand gripping

her throat indicated that she was unwell. She didn't try to slip the newspaper out of Consiglio's hands as she did when she wanted to tease him for fun. Nor did she go and find Lucia to persuade her to play 'queen's footsteps', a magical game in which her brothers could also take part. She particularly liked it when Lucia was the queen and she had her face to the wall with her eyes shut, which meant that she would only order lion steps or, if possible, grasshopper leaps. The game consisted of short ant steps or long lion ones, grasshopper leaps or crayfish steps as decreed by the queen to each of the players, after they had in turn uttered the ritual formula: 'O royal queen, your majesty, your loyal subjects greet thee, how many steps are we to take before we come and meet thee?' Then Lucia would order her brothers, who had long legs, to take one or two ant steps, finishing up with crayfish steps, while Mariuccia, with two lion steps and two grasshopper leaps, reached her in a moment and touched her arm: at that point she was able to assume the position of the queen.

That morning she did none of that but instead, walking on with her hand gripping her throat, she stopped near the hearth and didn't move again.

'Consiglio, go and call the doctor right now,' Custoda said to her husband, shaking him by an arm.

'What's going on?' he asked, as if speaking into the air, because Custoda had already rejoined Mariuccia.

Troubled by his wife's tone of voice, Consiglio rested his eyes on his daughter for a moment. Her mother had laid her out on two wicker chairs pushed together to form a little bed. He went over and touched her forehead; never before had he felt skin so scorching. Yes, they needed to go and get the doctor.

While she was preparing to go out, she assessed the situation. The road towards the village was all uphill and would take at least an hour to walk, but she had no alternative because the old mule wouldn't support her weight.

'Custoda, I'll go, and I'll be back as soon as possible. Meanwhile, why don't you give Mariuccia the herbal drink that you buy at the fair?'

'It's bitter, she's never wanted it.'

'It's a healthy drink. It even says so in the paper; there was a great big advertisement for it last week.'

'She can't swallow anything, not even water.'

'But the drink will do her good. Try it.'

'I told you she can't swallow anything. Do stop.'

'If you'd bought the drink it would have been fine, but because I bought it the drink is bad, and no one takes it.'

'Go and fetch the doctor. There's no time to lose.'

Consiglio looked at his daughter again, and again he felt her forehead. He had never seen that colour, so terrible a colour in a child. He was haunted by a dark presentiment.

He covered the first stretch of road swiftly, as if he had the strength of a little boy in his legs. It was such a steep climb that he tried not to think of anything but the journey; one step after the other, and he managed to hoist himself powerfully up there. Then he started running out of breath and was forced to slow down and a short time later to stop. He looked around: the road, already potholed and uneven, was densely filled with brambles, nettles and weeds. In the verge there were all kinds of animal droppings, cooked and blackened by the sun. He decided to take off everything that might slow his pace, the obstacles that impeded his movements. And since he was wearing only a jacket, he took that off and rolled it up under his arm. At one point it seemed to him that everything was upside down, and for a moment his mind was confused too. Death was revolting, in fact he had always imagined it old and wrinkled. But now why had his daughter, who was so small, suddenly turned that colour?

He arrived in the village in an hour, as predicted. With one last effort he arrived in the square and by the door of Dr Vesi, the only doctor in Alento. He knocked. No reply. He knocked again. Nothing.

Then he sat down on the steps, determined to wait until the doctor came back. A few minutes passed and the front door opened.

'Who are you?' an old woman's voice addressed the man slumped on the steps.

'Consiglio Parisi.'

'And what do you want?'

'I'm looking for the doctor. My daughter is ill.'

'Dr Vesi isn't here, he's left on a journey.'

'What do you mean, left?'

'Left left.'

'And when will he be back?'

'Not less than a week.'

'A week? I can't wait a week.'

'Listen, what can I tell you, Dr Vesi isn't here. But if you wait for him to finish his house calls, you could speak to Dr Paglia, from Cerre, who's standing in for Vesi.'

'Cerre, you said? But that's miles away. How am I supposed to get there?'

'What are you talking about? Dr Paglia is standing in for Vesi here in Alento, in his surgery. Wait for him right where you are now. As soon as he gets back, talk to him and he'll give you some medicine. Have you got any money?'

'Yes, signora, I have some money, but I would need to bring the doctor home to show him the child.'

'Where do you live?'

'In Terzo di Mezzo.'

'And do you have a way of bringing the doctor all the way down there?'

'No, signora.'

'Ah, some fine demands you people make. And yet none of this has anything to do with me. Listen to what the doctor tells you and you'll be fine.'

Consiglio stayed on the steps and started thinking of a dozen vague words, all in a row, that he would have to say to the doctor to persuade him to follow him all the way down there on foot. Beyond the steps he could just make out the voices of passers-by. He counted them one by one, a hundred times, to dispel the ghosts that tormented him from all sides. Every now and again he heard the cries of a little boy speeding through the square and ending up on the ground along with his scooter. Consiglio didn't know exactly what sort of thing children suffered from because it had always been the wife's task to take care of them, he just knew that a few years before he had risked losing Gianni, his third-born, who had been born pale and with his eyes closed like a pit-pony's. Only the sure movements of the midwife had managed to bring him back to life, her hands throwing cold water in his face, his little body shaking. That shaking. Gianni would repeat it in the years to come, in the attacks that came like electric shocks, always sudden and always after a brief tremor. The flashes of light that he always said he had seen would go with him throughout his life, which would come to an end just before he turned forty.

Paglia arrived at noon, weary from the number of house calls he had had to make so far.

'Who are you?' he asked Consiglio, as soon as he saw the bulk of his body on the steps.

'Consiglio Parisi,' he replied, and it was the second time that morning that he had said his name.

'Pleased to meet you, but what do you want? Don't make me waste my time, because I'm tired and in a hurry.'

Consiglio hesitated, unwilling to get his words wrong, even though he had repeated them over and over again to himself in the three hours that he had been waiting.

'Come on,' Paglia pressed.

'Doctor, it's about my daughter Mariuccia. She's very ill.'

'Are you all falling to pieces in this village? This morning alone I've been to ten houses. You should all get away from this malarial pit, before you get eaten alive. Tell me, what's up with your daughter?'

'She can't swallow anything, she's holding her hand around her throat and she doesn't speak.'

'Right, let's see her, where is she?'

'She's at home, with her mother. It wasn't a good idea to bring her to the village, we live in Terzo di Mezzo.'

'Fine. You're saying that I should come all the way down there with you on foot to see her?'

'There's no other way, I don't know what else to do.'

'Visits to far-off locations cost double, you know that?'

'Don't worry, I'll give you whatever you ask.'

'Double what I would take for a visit in the village. You've got the money?'

'Yes, doctor.'

'Fine. Give me a minute to get some medication from the surgery and let's go.'

Consiglio's journey back was much easier, not so much because of that as because of the presence of the doctor who was bound to be able to confront the danger that Mariuccia faced. Besides, a doctor is a bit like the hand of God, he thought, which settles on the heads of the stricken and heals them by searching inside their bodies, into those recesses that mere mortals can never enter.

Lost among these thoughts, without a jacket and with his shirt sleeves rolled up, Consiglio felt filled with a sense of wellbeing. 'Everything adjusts,' he said in an almost oracular tone, without turning round to anyone in particular, just to the void in front of him. Paglia, who was behind him struggling to keep up, asked him more than once to stop so that he could get his breath back, but Consiglio didn't hear anything. In less than an hour they had reached the house and Custoda, who had spent the morning between Mariuccia's bedside and the front door, was waiting for them.

'How is she?' her husband asked.

'Worse and worse,' she replied, looking at the doctor.

As soon as they got into the house, Paglia wrinkled his nose at the stench of smoke that filled it. He wasn't used to fireplaces, he hated them, being of the view that majolica stoves like the ones never seen in peasant homes were safer and more hygienic. Mariuccia was lying on two wicker chairs. A tepid stream flowed from her eyes to her neck, drenching her nightdress. The doctor bent over her body, while the others stood and waited.

'It's a lump in her throat,' he said, taking off his stethoscope as soon as the picture was clear.

'Is it serious, doctor?' asked Consiglio, who had also had lumps in his throat but who had tearfully waited for them to dissolve, hidden from everyone.

'A lump can either progress benignly or do the exact opposite. We can't know whether your daughter's lump is benign or not. In the event of doubt, we will have to take her to hospital. You know how to get there?'

'We have to go up to the main street. The owner of the general store has a hire car which I will ask him for, to take us all the way to town,' Consiglio replied. 'Do you think the child is fit to face such a long journey?'

'I'll give her an injection to enable her to face it more easily, but I can't do anything more than that. I will go with you to the general store and then carry on to Alento, because I have a very full day ahead of me. You're all falling to bits in this village.'

'How much do I owe you for your trouble?' Consiglio asked him, with a nervous glance.

'Drop by at the surgery tomorrow and we'll sort it out,' Paglia replied, taking from his bag a syringe and a box of medicines. Then he said, 'Prepare the child.'

Consiglio walked over to Mariuccia and lifted her up the way one might pick up a cat. The child was trembling and couldn't speak. Custoda hurried to take Mariuccia from her father's arms.

'Sit up,' she said, 'the doctor's going to give you an injection and you'll be better straight away.'

Paglia tugged Mariuccia's arm to free it from the sleeve, rubbed an area with cotton wool soaked in alcohol and slipped the needle into the first vein that seemed suitable. Mariuccia wobbled, but only a little. Having removed the needle, Custoda held her tightly in her arms and wrapped her in a blanket. Then she looked at her husband. 'I'm coming too,' she said, and he didn't object.

A short while later they were walking towards the

general store in silence. Paglia walked quickly ahead, with the Parisis just behind him, Mariuccia in her mother's arms.

The road was a rocky desert interrupted only by a few paths strewn with dead leaves. Occasional flinty tracks led off to the side, but they ignored them. At one point Paglia spat out an enormous beetle and cursed the insect that had flown into his mouth.

They had almost reached the main street when Custoda heard a wail, a faint groan like that of someone who is too weary to groan more loudly. She rested her eyes on Mariuccia: her head was caught in a beam of light, and her dry lips were pressed tightly together. She impulsively touched her face, then took her cheeks and pressed them together. 'Mariuccia, Mariuccia wake up.'

The child didn't move.

'Doctor, she's not breathing,' Custoda cried, and knelt on the ground with the child in her arms.

Startled, Paglia turned around. It was all happening to him today. He approached the child, shook her once or twice and then freed her from the blanket that she was wrapped in. He put his ear to her chest, no longer shaken by her troubled breathing; he put his ear to her mouth and the hiss of her breath had disappeared. Under the sleeve of her nightdress, at the exact point where he had given her the injection, the arm had swollen and pressed itself against the weave of the fabric; so had her little chest.

Mariuccia was dead, Paglia concluded, but not of a lump in her throat.

Night fell on the Parisis. The child was still in the arms of her mother, who was holding her tightly, as if to merge her daughter's flesh with her own, when Consiglio snatched the child from her and, taking her by her little hips, held her a precise distance from his eyes, as he did with his newspaper in the morning. He leaned his head first to one side and then the other, and now Mariuccia's face, covered with her hair, in fact looked more like a dandelion clock that had given up its wounded grace to the wind and was now depleted.

'Custoda, she isn't dead! Mariuccia isn't dead! She's pretending because she's a sly one. Custoda, do you hear me? Mariuccia is alive. She's trying to make a fool out of me to get hold of some chocolate. Mariuccia, open your eyes, Papa's going to give you chocolate. Custoda, you have a word, she believes in you. You have a look too, doctor. Where are you? Mariuccia is alive, come and see.'

Staring at the ground, Paglia was standing a little apart from the others, and as soon as he could not be seen he opened his bag. Between the stethoscope and the bottle of alcohol there were two boxes of medicine, almost identical, one of analgesics that he had hastily picked up from his surgery and the other digitalis in case of heart attacks. He studied them both, and the box of analgesics was as intact as it had been when he put it in the bag. He had used the wrong box. He had given Mariuccia an injection of digitalis and finished her off. Still staring at the ground, he walked over to Consiglio, who was now sitting on the ground holding his daughter's little body out in front of him. Custoda, in the middle of the road, was still on her knees, her arms dangling, as if carved from stone.

'Signor Parisi, I have to tell you something.'

'Doctor, you look too: Mariuccia's playing a prank, she's a cunning one.'

'No, Parisi, the child isn't pretending. Listen to me: I gave your daughter the wrong injection, I got the boxes of vials mixed up, they were almost the same, they were both new, and in short the digitalis will have given her a heart attack. I don't know what to tell you, I'm sorry.'

'I don't understand, doctor. What did you say?'

'I was very tired this morning. You're all falling to bits in this village. I gave the child one injection instead of another one. Distraction, that's all.'

'Distraction?'

'Yes, you don't imagine I did it on purpose? It was an error, caused by tiredness and darkness, because   you must admit – your house doesn't even have a light, you live on the ground floor and you still have lamps. Like animals.'

Like animals. Those were his precise words. Consiglio slowly got back to his feet and went and stood in front of him.

'Can you repeat that?'

'Are you deaf? I said that if you people didn't live like animals, without light and without the grace of God, I wouldn't have got the vials mixed up. That's what I said. Oh, that's enough, do what you want,' and with a brusque movement he began to leave.

It was at that point that Consiglio felt that he could no longer control not only his thoughts but his movements as well. He threw himself at the doctor's throat, thrusting his face against his face and looming over him with all his great bulk, with a passion so deranged that Paglia was startled.

'What are you trying to do, kill me?'

'You killed my daughter?'

'I could have avoided telling you about the wrong injection. You'd never have known. You must at least appreciate the honesty.'

'The honesty? You killed my daughter.'

'I was honest enough to tell you. I could have pretended nothing was wrong and told you that your daughter had died of a lump in the throat. You would have believed it. I would have made you believe it.'

'Give me back my daughter, you bastard. Who's going to repay me for a dead daughter, who's going to repay me?'

'Oh, I get it. You want money. The poor will accept anything for a handful of coins. How much do you want? Tell me and let's have done with it, because I've had a hell of a day today.'

'I will report you to the police, doctor, you can forget your handful of coins. I will report you.'

'You can do what you like, I've already told you. It'll be my word against yours. But you should know that I will admit nothing, and you have no witnesses. I, on the other hand, have at least two or three colleagues who owe me kindnesses. They will testify in my favour about the death of your daughter, whenever I ask them.'

'There's no one here, just us. Who can testify falsely in your favour?'

'How naive you are! I'm a doctor, a luminary, born into a feared and respected family of doctors. You, on the other hand, are merely an idiot, the son of idiots and the father of more idiots. Nobody pays any attention to people like you in the street, let alone in court.'

For a moment Consiglio's mind was fogged. He couldn't have said how, but he found himself gripped by a flash of memory that took him to a few years before, when his wife was involved in the trial over Micchetto's land. Custoda had always said that her accuser's testimony was false, a blatant lie, but he hadn't believed her, or at least that was what he had said to her.

'The law is above all things, my dear doctor, even luminaries and powerful families. You won't get away with it,' and he said it all in a single breath, without weighing his words, but he knew that this was also wrong.

'Ah, ah, ah,' and with each of his ah's Paglio raised the tone of his voice, 'the law is made by men for men, not by a God in heaven without any interest in earthly things. And since all men have a price, my dear Parisi, all we need to do is establish the sum.'

Consiglio was perfectly alert to the warning contained in the words. He looked around as if to get his breath back and fixed his eyes on the little gravel path that hugged the road and led to his cousin Pietro's farm. Further along, almost hidden, there was a white willow that was swathed in ivy and had assumed the creeper's colour. Every time he visited his cousin he stopped and looked at it. It was said that the willow had healed the sick and wounded of the Great War who had returned to the village, before welcoming in its soil those who had not survived. Then the ivy had embraced it and, entwined like that, they had learned to survive together, in each other's thrall even in darkness. At night they could be seen asleep, together in a common weariness.

'Go now, doctor, get out of here. No one will be able to help idiots like me, not even the law, you're right. But people like you will have to face the judgement of history.'

Consiglio wasn't entirely clear what he meant by those three phrases, constructed with the bare minimum of words, but he liked the sound he had made. He turned towards his wife, who was still kneeling perfectly still where he had left her, then he looked at his daughter's body, caught in one last ray of sunlight but now consigned to an eternity of death. He lifted it from the ground, wrapping it in the blanket that seemed still to hold her warmth, and walked over to his wife. Custoda looked at him, and in that look there were centuries of grief that had somehow been swallowed down. He held out a hand to her and she took it. Both standing, they hugged. They had never done that before, even at moments of necessary intimacy, consummated hastily and only to warm themselves on seemingly endless nights. But now, in the grief that gripped them, they could finally let go because that kind of contact no longer caused them shame. Hugging like that as they hugged their daughter – they hadn't even hugged their children, filling their lives with solitude – they slowly made their way home. The sun had clearly gone mad, because it reappeared, only to accompany them on their journey.

Estella

It's just before nine. The clock ticks groggily, more slowly than usual. As I wait, I flick through an old calendar full of old photographs showing images of the village when it wasn't yet a pile of stones, when people lived there and I was about to go back, renouncing forever my perceptions of the world outside.

One of those faded photographs shows the square, with its big elm tree, and the church with its facade still intact. It was a fine morning but the big square had already turned into a bog: the earth was falling, and it had been falling for some time. The faces of the few houses around the square were already chapped by the wind, of which there has never been a shortage here. In the background, on the edge of the square, you can glimpse Maccabeo's general store and, sitting outside, there he is, tiny in the distance, indefatigable, as he records something in one of his accounting books.

When I got back to the village, the shutter of the general store was already lowered and rusty. Maccabeo had grown old, but he had never stopped waiting for his children's return.

The return. I imagined my own as a plunge into a river, not knowing whether it was calm or not. But then the sky looked gently down and for a moment I had a family that replaced my missing memories and calmed the river, into which I dived without thinking, with the little swells of water holding me up. Now that it's all done, I know what river I've ended up in.

If I look around, the night fills me with its fearful procession of shadows, and every time, every time, I refuse to let go without a struggle. It's in those moments that I wonder, as if by way of consolation, if the village was there or if the village was a dream, if it was only a magical imposture. But, vague though it is in memory, I know that it existed and that it lives on and wanders slowly in the remaining light, a light with a patina of ancient Greece that strikes the crumbled facades, the debris-lined edges of the sloping streets, the cemetery of the lonely and the many, dispersed around scattered and swollen graves.

When they arrive I will welcome them with an 'Ooh', as if I'm surprised to see them, as if the visit is unexpected. At first they will pay me no attention and try to look outside, to search for the old elm tree in the square, a boundless mass of green, a hirsute and dishevelled fury that presents itself to the eye like a stand-in for time. Meanwhile the moon will have begun to shine, its light passing through the cracks in the window, made visible by the dancing specks of dust. In that moment, in the silence that will give form to revelation, the wind will rise but like a breath that no one hears. Year after year, events play out in precisely this sequence, yet my trepidation ahead of the moment is undiminished. Now, for example, I would happily smoke a pipe, if I smoked.

Maccabeo

Alento was not just the land of solitary farmers plunging rakes into their little fields, or the few members of the gentry who lived apart from the others. There were also the tenant farmers, who went on building and investing in spite of the fact that the land beneath their feet was crumbling like the side of a mountain.

Old Vincenzo Maccabei – Maccabeo to everyone, all the time – was one of those tenant farmers. Slim and tireless, he had launched a business selling fabrics and gold objects, and things had immediately gone well. The shop he opened in the village prospered unexpectedly, which meant that he was able to expand by opening another to the rear, this one specialising in chamber pots, handkerchiefs and teaspoons.

Commercial activities involve making sacrifices but bring respectability and money. They also brought Maccabeo wider perspectives, now that his two sons had grown up and their careers were beginning to take shape.

Antonio, the first-born, had an aptitude for commerce, and his loquaciousness would soon bring the desired results. Luchino, meanwhile, lived and studied in the capital as a tenant in the luxurious house of Signora Iolanda, originally from Alento. Over the course of a year, the boy, who wrote home regularly, would be awarded his degree; then, with some guidance from his brother, he would refine his business sense, and he too was bound to prosper, given that none of the other industrialists of Alento had studied as much as he did.

'A house with such sons is a rich house,' Maccabeo said to his wife in the evening, as he sank into his damask armchair and, full of love for his family, read and re-read the cards sent by Luchino, his eyes as bright as if reading an illustrated magazine.

'Does he want more money?' she asked, with that hint of detachment and resignation that irritated Maccabeo, who, unlike his wife, was swollen with pride over Luchino's news and felt most satisfied.

'Yes, but what does that have to do with anything? Living in the capital isn't like living in Alento, there are expenses. You, my dear, I'm sorry to say, have an impoverished spirit, you don't know what it means to have initiative, you don't know the importance of being appreciated by others. If Luchino spends his money on Camparis and *cicchetti* for his friends, I'm just saying, then that will prove useful in future. The *cicchetti* that he gives his friends today are a way of shoring up respectability for the future.'

'I think you should keep a closer eye on him,' she interrupted, cutting him off, overwhelmed with boredom.

Anna Maccabeo had an ancient and persistent belief in predestination. There were pitfalls enough, she believed, when it came to business, when it came to getting things done or importing things from elsewhere, chamber pots, for example, to sell to the people who worked the land. She didn't come from a poor family, it wasn't that; her family had always had shoes to wear, gentlemanly shoes that made a faint shuffling sound. Yet no one could convince her that each person's place was not the one assigned by fate. That it had been revealed from birth, one that happened in a certain place and not in another; which was why the career of a young man born in Alento – whether his father was a peasant or a businessman made no difference – was marked from the outset compared to that of a contemporary born, even in modest circumstances, in Rome or Paris, or even New York. Something that was demonstrated by the emigration routes, which always followed a single direction: from Alento into the unknown, and not the other way round, which must have meant something.

'Oh my dear, can't you try not to see everything in the worst possible light?' Maccabeo said to her, bringing his plump hands to his face, soft hands, as he himself never tired of pointing out. 'I suppose I ended up digging the fields like my father did? I had courage, and the miracle that dragged me from the land occurred thanks to my intelligence, my entrepreneurialism, of which I have plenty.'

'Your entrepreneurialism involved in selling chamber pots?' she said, as if delivering the *coup de grâce*.

'They too are useful, my dear. Don't forget, I also sell silver teaspoons,' Maccabeo replied, not even slightly offended. 'But the point is a different one,' he carried on calmly, very calmly, in fact, clasping his hands over his slightly inflated belly. 'I have always believed that even if the birds of the air live in the fields that's no reason for me to do the same. When I go out in the morning, nicely dressed, and stroll towards the square; when I pass through the doorway of my shops and think about what's behind me, where I've just been, I put on my unpatched jacket and breathe out beatifically.'

'The fact that you've done well doesn't mean your sons will,' she said, giving herself little pointless taps on the legs just in order to do something. 'Times have changed. Far away from here there's a war on, but you don't seem to be aware of that. Soon your sons will be called up too.'

'You put it very well: the war is far away. It is a matter of nation-states and hidden motives that need not concern us.

They concern Antonio and Luchino even less. They are our sons, they don't belong to the war. And there's one other thing: did we bring them up for war? I directed their gaze beyond the fields, towards the sea, towards progress. Abandon your defeatism, it will do us no good.'

'The war is a matter for everyone. That much is proved by the call-up cards, which are also arriving here, to remind us,' she concluded, speaking faster each time to show the mettle of her mind, resigned yet smug, as she prepared to go to bed, leaving her husband to his pointless speeches.

'Progress doesn't stand still, even if there's a war on somewhere else,' poor Maccabeo said with one final explosive burst, not noticing that his wife was no longer there. 'It runs and runs on unpredictable tracks, sometimes risky, but always heading towards modernity. Are you listening to me? My sons, besides inheriting their intelligence and entrepreneurial spirit from me, have studied, they know the traps that lie hidden in words. You'll see, my dear, their paths will be smooth. You'll see.' And with these words, as if he had both his sons in front of him, he smiled and nodded, his arms held wide in a gesture of blessing.

Vincenzo Maccabei looked straight ahead with the strength of a constant springtime, following his path and pursuing it as best he could.

His progress had never faced impediments because he had never placed his trust in anyone else, let alone in fate. His chief resource had always been represented by himself; he had taken charge of his destiny and never, really never, been subjected to it. And since the world belongs to those who know how to conquer it, he had started from Alento, an outpost of boundaries, a bass drum set down on a grassy

plain destined to dissolve into the earth; but his sons
would go much further, they needed only to be given time.

Taranto, 14 April 1916

Dearest Father,

I am writing to assure you of my excellent state
of health, and to wish the same for all of you.
As regards my brother, I don't know if he sat his
exams or not, maybe you can tell me. I learned from
Naples that you were sent a sample of chamber
pots, did you receive it? As to the chest cloths.
I will send them if I can. Please note that the prices
on all articles have increased to an extraordinary
degree. I am keeping company with many whole-
sale dealers, and they keep me up to date with
everything. Perhaps we will manage to get together
at Easter, I very much hope so.

My greetings and warmest embraces to
everyone.

Yr. aff. son Antonio

Taranto, 25 April 1916

Dearest Father,

I sent a letter yesterday, I expect you have already
received it. I also saw Luchino at Salerno station and
thought he looked very well, very elegant. You won't
mind that he plans to leave Salerno soon. He needs
to study, I have recommended as much, don't worry.
If he spends more than he should, pretend you sent
it to me, and I will find a way. I arrived here this
morning, after an excellent journey. Tell Mother
not to worry.

Greetings and embraces to you all.

Yr. aff. son Antonio

Taranto, 12 May 1916

Dearest Father,

I was pleased to receive your letter learning that you are all well. As for me, Taranto is no longer a war zone, they have taken the daily half-lira away from us and are giving us two soldi as before. They have stopped giving us wine and our rations are reduced as well. For our daily correspondence they charge us at least ten soldi. You will forgive me if at present I cannot write to you every day. If they grant me leave, I could be with you on the 15 inst. When I arrive, we will meet the person from Salerno and see if we can conclude the deal.

Greetings and embraces to you all.

Yr. aff. Son Antonio

Taranto, 31 July 1916

Dearest Father,

2 August is my birthday, and I request that you be cheerful and spend the day as if I were at home. Please make a note of what is happening in the fabric store, look in the buttons and see if there are any missing, because I am expecting a travelling salesman from Naples and I would like to award him the commission. Let me know if Baron La Rocca is coming to Alento as I was told. Please find out. Did you receive the garlands? If you have an opportunity to see Mr Ermenegildo, tell him that he and his sister can keep the money ready.

Dearest embraces and kisses to all.

Yr. aff. son Antonio

Taranto, 26 August 1916

Dearest Father,

I am writing to assure you that I am very well, and hope that the same is true of all of you. Arriving in Taranto I asked whether our villagers, who were part of recruitments 63 and 64, were still here. I was assured that they had left.

Please assure Signora Palmieri that I will give her the parcel she entrusted to me via her husband as soon as I see her. Also tell Signora Maria that I was unable to entrust the letter to Tanino because he had already left when I went to see him. You don't know how sorry I am that my brother is unable to sit his exams, but I imagine that everything he told us was nonsense. I won't keep you any longer. Before I am granted leave I will write again.

Yr. aff. son Antonio

Taranto, 28 September 1916

Dearest Father,

I sent a letter last Sunday and told you I had sent the package of handkerchiefs. But in the end I didn't send the package, so don't worry if it didn't reach you. I received the card with news of Luchino. I took great pleasure in learning that he has been assigned to the Terzo Genio regiment, and particularly that he is leaving for Florence. I hope he will sit his exams and know how to do his duty.

I am well as I hope you all are too.

Yr. aff. son Antonio

Taranto, Batteria Ciuria, 14 November 1916

Dearest Father,

I am writing in reply to your last. I am aware that
you have spent every day waiting for me, but what
do you expect me to do? I haven't come yet because
we're waiting for people to go on farming leave.
I'll talk to you about other things when I turn up.
That's likely to be on the 20th of this month or the
24th. I am aware that others have been called up,
but don't make too much of it: they aren't being
called up because there have been losses, but
because there is a need for new batteries to be
placed in taken positions by way of reinforcement
and to avoid losing an inch of the territory we've
taken, that's all. When I come to see you we will
talk about lots of things and ascertain the lay of the
land. I hope you've brought in a considerable sum.
Give as little credit as possible, and only to those
who deserve it.

Hugs and kisses to everyone.

Your son Antonio

Just two knocks at the door, on a morning like any other,
and the war entered Maccabeo's house as well. It was an
extremely hard blow. All kinds of strategies were devised to
prevent their departure, but to no avail. Maccabeo had even
tried to hide them, first one and then the other, in spite
of the ignominy that would have resulted. But the old man
wasn't afraid of that kind of shame, since deserting from

the front line – a front line that no one in Alento had ever heard mentioned – was a legitimate, almost dutiful act. Had he perhaps brought up his sons to send them to die far from home? Had he raised them on white bread and meat – a considerable quantity of meat, to satisfy an ancient hunger that was more his than theirs – for a phantom fatherland that had until then been seemingly unaware of Alento's existence? It was all too convenient, waiting till now to discover this forgotten outpost, just to turn it into a storehouse of young flesh to be sent to the slaughter.

Maccabeo had seldom uttered the word 'Italy' in his life, and he had never managed to feel part of it. He did, however, feel part of his sons' lives. He had brought them up well and sent them to study, waiting for the miracle of seeing them walk safely along the path of progress, ahead of what were now his old man's footsteps. And now the fatherland, the land of fathers who were not his own, had come to spoil the path he had traced out.

Antonio was the first to leave, destined for the port of Taranto, where he stayed for a year; then he was sent to the front.

Luchino's departure, a short time later, was preceded by a revelation that old Maccabeo found almost more painful than the threat of the front. His son – that gifted son of his, on whom he had placed so many of his expectations, his Luchino who had graduated from grammar school with excellent marks and then continued without a break – he was the one who had abruptly decided to break off his studies, without mentioning it to anyone, let alone his father. And that wasn't all: the registered letters that Maccabeo had sent him over the past year so that he might cut a fine figure among his city friends, he had used only to dedicate himself to women and personal excess. At one point he had even stopped paying his rent to Signora Iolanda.

When Luchino confessed what he had done, Maccabeo was aware of blood rising into his eyes, which were raised to the heavens as if in a spasm, and then for a few moments his heart ceased to pump. To keep from falling he grabbed on to his wife, who took advantage of the moment to start up her litany of I-told-you-so's.

Maccabeo didn't give up straight away, because it was still possible that Luchino had been distracted by some of those hopeless characters who came from the villages and were seeing the world for the first time. Bad company, he had always believed, can infect a promising existence more disastrously than a weed in a well-sown field. A few weeks of rest in the warmth of his house, sheltered from temptations, would certainly do him good; a month, two at the most, of healthy living, decent food and paternal affection would lead him to reconsider. Luchino didn't have to do anything but resume his studies, and Maccabeo would take care of everything else, particularly given that he was all he had left now that Antonio had gone.

Except that almost immediately Luchino's papers had arrived as well, on two crinkled sheets: the fatherland was calling him up, even though he was little more than a boy; it was summoning him to send him to his death.

Consumed with anxiety, Maccabeo had no option but to accept what was happening. Once both his sons had gone, the days grew shorter, the autumn wind and rain laid waste to the resting countryside. Maccabeo stood by the window and surprised himself by staring at the leafless trees. It was years since he had last paid attention to the changing seasons, because his work did not respond to the cycles of nature, hail or thunderstorms. Many years of life locked away in his work had granted him an infallible gift of rationality, succinct and logical, not in any way influenced by imponderables. A form of reasoning that could be summed up in a single word: 'act'. Now, however, he knew that the Molzone boys would stay in Alento because they were farmers, as were the Corlano lads. Peasants all, and all excused military service for that very reason.

In the *Giornale della Provincia*, an anonymous editorialist had written that *if the charming public service of the Post and Telegraph did not exist (bringing, as it does, so much to us and to the coffers of state), our mild, patient and most principled local public would not even notice that the nation is at war. Where, in fact, is the roar of battle, where the rumble of columns of trucks, where the heavy carriages of the formidable batteries of war?*

Even much later, Maccabeo would read and re-read that editorial. Antonio's letters arrived with a certain regularity, and there was no mention of war in those postcards that were sent post-free from the front, like messages from nowhere. He tried to read between the lines, knowing that they had been censored, but try as he might he couldn't read anything in them other than Antonio's concerns about failed business deals, and about his being far from home.

The war drew near only when telegrams arrived with news of the fallen, but the dismay lasted only a moment, because on the face of it nothing seemed to have changed – there were no food shortages, for example. And even when the *Giornale della Provincia* announced a defeat and listed the numbers of the dead, how could that news seem true when it appeared alongside advertisements for a hairdresser offering the latest Parisian styles, or just above an account of the ennoblement of Cavalier Riboldi?

Maccabeo remembered that in 1914, a time of political neutrality, the newspaper was filled with articles rejecting the war. Now, on the other hand, even the most ardent advocates of neutrality accepted the reasons set out for it in the name of the necessity of a fatherland embodied by the king, around which, according to the newspaper, they needed to rally. *Italy at this hour feels not only the tremor of war but a great impulse of love, which with its flame melts together spirits, plans and hopes.* If Maccabeo felt an impulse of love it was only for his sons, destined to die in some corner of a foreign field. His plans and hopes, like the plans and hopes of thousands of faceless and nameless others, did not coincide with the tremor of war: was it possible that no one had the courage to say so? Perhaps the journalists did say it, the ones whose articles had been censored with wide white spaces between the lines; examples of last-minute censorship now exposed with no comment from the editorial team.

If the general state of things was a unanimous acceptance of the conflict, in line with the grand designs of conquest on the part of the nation-states, Maccabeo remained convinced that the level of his own personal history, different from the rest and ignored by governments, clashed with the levels of a larger story whose meaning escaped him, if there was a meaning in being killed or freezing to death by the hundreds.

He responded to the confusion whirling around him by being permanently on the brink of sleep. He began to prepare for silence by going and standing by the window, waiting for letters from his sons. Sometimes he would fall asleep standing up, his heart tender. At other times he would stare at the hearth, glancing hopefully upwards every time a dog barked: 'No, there are no cards today,' the postman would reply woundingly. Days without news were lost days, and they slipped by Maccabeo without his noticing. His wife thought he had entered a cloud of madness; in fact he had become a void hovering between life and death.

Taranto, 2 December 1916
Dearest Father,
I should like to tell you that I am enjoying good health, and hope that you are too. I have had nothing so far and am still waiting to be granted leave. I am living on hunches, but have patience. The classes of '76 and '77 third category have been called up, and within days the same will happen to all of those declared unfit from between '76 and '81; then it appears that mobilisation will be complete. I bet there's no one left in the village. What joy. I hope to be with you for Christmas. It's possible that our Luchino will be there too. I would ask you to draw a veil over my brother's past and devote your attention to him rather than to me, because he's so young and not as good at adapting to life as I am. Have patience with his past whims. Soon you will be learning important things about the war, I can't tell you about it now.
Greetings to all,
Yrs, Antonio

Taranto, 10 March 1917
Dearest Father,
I should like to reassure you that the steamer you mention was entirely full of French soldiers, so

don't worry about me or Luchino. If he hasn't
written to you yet, he will. He has always been a
lazy one.

Hugs and salutations,
Yr. aff. son Antonio

Taranto, 29 April 1917
Dearest Father,
I have received your precious letter and am
hurrying to reply: don't worry about my brother's
laziness. I will write to him today and reproach him
for not writing. I imagine that things are not well
with you, given that I haven't heard from you for so
long. Don't worry, there is no rush. The important
thing is that you are well.

Warmest greetings, hugs,
Yr. aff. son Antonio

War zone, 8 May 1917
Dearest Father,
I should like to assure you that I am in the best
of health. The climate here is fine at this time
of year, we are surrounded by white mountains.
Why do you not write to me if you've cashed in
the promissory notes? I know that your plan is
not to hurt anyone because they are all fathers,
but you could at least calculate the interest
due to us. Tell me more about the shops, do you
really plan to close them? I hope not. Frankly
I would lease them out if you can get a good
price. Oh for the day when I am able to do my
own business!

We need only pray to God to bring an end to
the war so that I can come home soon.

Kisses to you all.

Yrs affly, Antonio

War zone, 3 August 1917

Dearest Father

Yesterday I was in the company of Eduarduccio
Conza. You can't imagine how pleased I was to
meet a fellow villager, as if I had seen my brother.
No news of Luchino, however. Since you ask about
the war, I am here to tell you: they are killing the
enemy bravely and steadfastly, in the direction
of Monte Santo. We are on the Alto Isonzo, on
territory that was once ours, which the barbarian
enemy robbed from us and which is now ours
once again.

I send you a thousand kisses.

Yrs aff. Antonio

War zone, 25 September 1917

My dearest ones,

I have received yours after a long delay. I ask you,
and Mother in particular, not to worry if you have
heard nothing from my brother. I can tell you why,
since I have found out. There has been no fighting
where he is, and if there had been, he was in a
safe place. The reason for the silence is that it is
difficult for postmen to negotiate those mountains.
And even though I have had no reply to the tele-
gram I sent to his unit, it doesn't mean anything.
I will write to the Ufficio Concentramento in

Bologna for information. Please do not build castles in the air.

> Hugs,
> Yrs, Antonio

Oriolo Romano, 14 January 1918
Dearest Father,

The two money orders reached me yesterday, thank you for being so thoughtful. I also thank you for the subscription for 500 cigarettes and for the 2 kg of bread. If there were a pair of shoes at home that you could possibly send to me, I would be very pleased because the shoes that I have weigh 5 kilos, so full are they of nails. Buying them here is impossible, because I would have to spend 50 lire. Still nothing from my brother. I never had a reply from Bologna either. I am uneasy, because bad news about the army is coming in every day. But please do not despair, and I won't either.

> Greetings and kisses,
> Yrs, Antonio

From the front, 8 June 1918
Dearest Father,

Forgive me if none of mine has reached you until now. How are you? All well here, always cheerful and never daunted, please don't worry: we have become bold warriors, I can say with head held high, and no longer draft-dodgers. I am in a barracks with the captain, don't worry about me. God will keep me from any danger,

the important thing is that our ancient enemy
is defeated.

    Kisses,
    Yrs aff. Antonio

    From the front, 28 June 1918
I'm writing in reply to your last precious letter.
I confirm that there has been a bombing raid that
lasted approximately 8 hours, everyone unharmed.
Still cheerful and undaunted, please don't worry:
we have become bold warriors, as we can say with
our heads held high, no longer draft-dodgers.

    Antonio

    War zone, 30 August 1918
    Dear Father,
Your precious letter has reached me. Please think
no more about Luchino. Great was his sacrifice
for the Fatherland, but necessary. Let us take no
more interest in the business, since the landslide
is devouring the premises. Always cheerful, never
daunted, please don't worry: we have become bold
warriors, as we can say with our heads held high,
and no longer draft-dodgers.

    Antonio

    War zone, 18 October 1918
    Dear Father,
We are here in the depths of winter, it's raining and
snowing, it's absolutely freezing, but I think it's
better here than where you are, given the epidemic
that's going about and the dangers of the landslide.

You say that a business deal collapsed. Have patience.
Always cheerful and never daunted, please don't
worry: we have become bold warriors, as we may say
with our heads held high, and no longer draft-dodgers.
    Antonio

    From the party field, 5 November 1918
    Dear Father,
I have run out of free postcards, which means
that I will be able to write less and less. When you
have the mass said for Luchino remember to light
a candle in my name. Always cheerful and never
daunted, please don't worry: we have become bold
warriors, as we may say with our heads held high,
and no longer draft-dodgers.
    Antonio

Part Three

The Dinner

Stretti tutti insieme,
insieme tutta la famiglia morta,
sotto il cipresso fumido che geme,

stretti così come alter sere al foco
(urtava, come un povero, alla porte
Il tramontano con brontolio roco),

piangono. La pupilla umida e pia
ricerca gli altri visi a uno a uno
e forma un'altra lagrima per via.

All huddled tightly together,
the whole dead family all together,
beneath the damp and groaning cypress tree,

huddled tightly together as on other fireside evenings
(knocking at the door like a beggar
the mountain wind with its rough roar),

they weep. The moist and pious eye
seeks the other faces one by one
and another tear forms along the way.

Giovanni Pascoli, *Il giorno dei morti*
(The Day of the Dead)

They have arrived. One after the other they have come in and arranged themselves around the table. Gideon has come in with them, calm at last, and curled up at the foot of the stove.

The first to come in was Lucia Parisi, in a stunning blue dress ruched just below the bosom, a wide skirt and puffed sleeves, the blue complicated by some silver threads. She has a tulle stole wrapped tightly around her neck, fastened at the front with a filigree brooch that looks like a butterfly. Thus bathed in a delicate glow, Lucia looks like a little flame of the kind you might see in a summer twilight, when the first stars appear.

For her, under the macramé napkin, there is a nice piece of chocolate, wrapped in tinfoil with a bow at the side; around it I have scattered raisins and berries. I hope in that way to make the present even more agreeable to her.

The next to appear was Cola Forti. Enormous, almost Homeric, his belly is uncontained, open to the pristine whiteness of his shirt. Looking more closely you can see that his waistcoat has no buttons, and neither does the shirt. It was his custom to pull them off because he couldn't bear them, but tonight, enclosed in a little jute bag, he will find them in his glass when he sits down at the table.

Now, with a resolute gait like that of an old soldier, in comes the good Maccabeo, followed by Libera Forte, who seems not to have seen her father, who came in just ahead of her. Maccabeo still has a long and dishevelled beard that bestows on him a certain slovenliness, but he is the most joyful of the company. He smiles affectionately at Libera, who is walking beside him, then turns to look at the others, and it is plain that he would hug everyone if they let him. Over the course of dinner he will try to give some of his food to the person sitting next to him, to establish a bond. When he lifts his plate, rather than a place mat he will find one of his accounting books, with a hard cover, the pages inside yellowed and all closely annotated with the figures and names of the merchandise.

Libera is still thin, and she seems to me to have grown slighter. Having rid herself of her ill-defined mourning, she is now wearing a rust-coloured flouncy dress, tight at the waist and with short sleeves, which is why she holds a woollen shawl folded under her arm, of a more vivid red even though the furbelows disperse the colour. She is carrying with her a piece of parchment on which she has written some lines of poetry and, before sitting down at the table, still standing behind her chair, she begins to read:

Our mother, exiled in heaven
Shallow be thy name.
Thy queendom come, at least before the grave
Thy will be done
In heaven certainly but on earth especially.
Give us this day our daily expectations
But give us also our bread
That we may eat in peace
And lead us into temptation
But may the bed be ours, and ours the quivers
    of the flesh.
And liberate us from mortal embraces,
As from the guilt that they have said is ours always.

Once she has sat down, she will find under her napkin the little glass bottle that guards the tooth she lost on her wedding night. The spirit in which it is immersed has preserved its enamel, and has also kept the little nerves, excised in the bump against the bar.

While Libera is declaiming, Giacinto arrives. Dressed up to the nines, he looks a fine young gentleman. There is no trace of his yellow teeth, he now has a new set of teeth. He comes in chewing, I see that his mouth is full of bread; now that he has teeth, he can have bread as well. He leans on a cherrywood stick, but only out of habit, because his eyes can now see. When he moves his chair away from the table, he will see on the chair the yellow braided cap: caught off guard, he won't be able to contain himself.

The last to come in is Consiglio Parisi, in a dark grey jacket and with his trousers held up by a length of wire. He still has his pitch-black eyes, and the severity with which he rests them on others is unaltered, like his rather unceremonious manners. He could have smartened himself up, but he preferred to stay as he was. He has an asthmatic wheeze, but it doesn't seem to trouble him. As far as he can, he approaches the window with the intention of squashing his face against the panes to look at the elm tree, which, heedless of us, seems to hold the moon in the embrace of its branches. It is at that moment that I run to half-close the shutters; Parisi looks at me askance, then moves aside and says: 'It's beautiful, our elm tree. It's all that remains of the village.'

'I know,' I agree, 'it was beautiful even then.'

By his place marker, Consiglio Parisi will find a lamp with an electric heart that looks like a mad lightning flash. It will remind him of the time of backwardness and the time of modernity, the period of darkness and the period of light.

As to the light in this room – which must be faint but sufficiently bright to see faces and hands – I have decided on a few candles and a small spirit lamp with a cotton wick. All together, they provide enough light for our needs.

We sit down without looking at each other very much and start staring at the tureen in the middle of the table, from which I will take the ricotta ravioli, after serving the antipasto.

A parrot-like voice from the back of the room announces the arrival of Marcello, who, as predicted, had no hesitation in joining us.

'Here I am again,' he says and sits down facing me.

Dinner can commence.

I serve an outstanding antipasto: slices of bread covered with an olive paste that I dried in the sun when the season was right and then reduced to a cream in the mortar.

The guests ask for something to drink. Water, cold water from the elm tree. I pour some for everybody and notice that Marcello is strangely silent.

'Marcello, tell us something,' I say.

'I don't know what to say.'

'What do you mean, you don't know what to say?' I ask, startled because he's never lost for words.

'I don't know what to say,' he repeats.

'That's impossible. You always have something to say.'

'I'd just like to know why you summon them.'

'I invite them to dinner, that's all,' I reply, and, looking at the guests covertly, I try to work out whether they're listening to us.

'You should leave them alone and think about the suffering you're causing.'

'For now I'm offering them a delicious meal.'

'And what have you made for me?'

'Antipasto, ricotta ravioli, stuffed figs. The same as everyone else.'

'I don't see anything,' he says, leaning back in his chair and spreading his arms in a gesture of surrender.

'Here we are again! When will you stop contradicting me?'

'Do you know what's in the tureen?' he asks me and leans forward again.

'Steaming ravioli that we will eat in a few moments,' I reply.

'White stones in a water broth,' he retorts.

'Oh come on! And the antipasto I just served you?'

'Wooden slats smeared with mud, which is not in short supply around here. You could at least have made me some zabaglione.'

'You won't have any this year. I haven't had time to make it.'

'But you have had time to wander from house to house in search of hateful souvenirs for your guests.'

'They'll be happy with them.'

'You think.'

'Fine, fine, I need it, I need them to come back. But I should add, they too need to come back, and to this house in particular. No one ever really wanted to leave,' and I start twirling a lock of my hair – still long and vaguely blonde – between my fingers.

'I admire the persistence with which you mask your interest with generosity. The truth is that you keep them prisoner because you feel alone and it's killing you,' he says in a voice with a hoarse edge to it and starts staring at the lock of hair that I have wrapped around a finger;

then he raises his eyes to mine and adds, 'and besides, I don't count.'

As he looks at me I feel trapped, a swiftly unravelling sweater caught on a thorn. I unwrap my hair from my finger to bring it to my mouth, as I used to do as a child when, barefoot and with my damp curls framing my face, I went in search of my mother, any mother would have done, to say to me: *So you're alive, you're alive.* 'Oh, Marcellino, what are you saying to me? At our age...' I say, lowering my eyes because I no longer want to look into his.

'Come away from this tomb. In my house you will have rooms all to yourself, I won't bother you.'

Leave me alone, I say to myself, will you leave me alone? Then to him: 'I have various rooms all to myself right here. I look at them day after day and they are smiling faces, with their toothless mouths, their ruffled heads. I go in, I climb perilous stairs, I am grateful to the walls that continue to hold.'

'The walls are rotten.'

'While the walls still stand, my guests exist. I keep them here with me and I take them back to their former lives.'

'But who says this is what they want? If you were less mean you would leave them in peace.'

'That's enough, Marcello. I'm tired of your insults. Get up and join me as I walk around the table: I have to check that the guests want for nothing, and more particularly that they have enjoyed my little gifts.'

'The usual ritual. We walk around the table as you do at wedding feasts, except that there are no feasts here, and certainly no wedding.' Marcello goes on insulting me, but now there's an almost melodious moan in his voice.

'Stop moaning and give me your arm,' I say at last, to keep him quiet.

In walking around the table, my chief concern is to see whether my guests are pleased with the presents I have given them. I stop for a moment behind each chair, leaning on Marcello's arm, which feels strong to me, even though it's only the effect of his grip, as if he were determined never to let me go. I try to guess the thoughts of the guests, I attempt to mediate between theirs and mine. I lend an ear to their whispers, to distinguish melancholy from a hint of contentment. How could they fail to draw pleasure from receiving presents?

'Do you think they appreciated it? They look petrified to me,' I eventually ask Marcello, who has for a moment interwoven his fingers with mine, the soft fingers of a man who has never worked, yet so reassuring.

'You should stop going into their houses.'

'They're open, I don't force the doors. And if the brambles are too thick and I can't get in, I rely on Gideon, who knows other ways in.'

'That's not the point. The point is that you take intimate objects out of their houses, to decorate the table with them out of mere mischief.'

'Oh, please do stop,' I say to him brusquely, pulling away.

I decide to serve the ricotta ravioli, which have an inviting appearance even without tomato sauce. I prefer to leave them *in bianco*, adorned only with the olive oil that I made myself. When the time is right – in October, more or less – I pick up the fruits at the feet of the olive trees that have survived in the strips of countryside where the village ends, and I take them down to the river, to the old olive press. In its day, the Alento olive tree produced exquisite oil in great abundance. The olive press, on the other hand, was a wheel that required women to turn it. 'We're obliged to do this,' the owner of several beautiful olive trees once said to me, 'because quadrupeds are *considerably more expensive* than bipeds.'

I serve the ravioli on the porcelain plates left to me by Ada de Paolis, along with the silver cutlery and the fine glass goblets with the gilded rims. The plates are white with a pattern of bright blue pagodas in the middle; before buying them, the de Paolis made certain that they came from China.

Everyone present concentrates on the steaming tureen, they are clearly very hungry. So I line up the ravioli – four or five per plate, not more – on the roofs of the blue-patterned pagodas. I prepare to observe my guests, as they immediately bend over their dishes.

'What was that hum of words, a little while ago?' Cola Forti says, turning to Consiglio Parisi.

'They were talking about memories, and of a dead village, a land that once was. Now it sits motionless over a big swamp,' he replies, dismissing with a wave of his hand the plate thrust in front of him by Maccabeo, trying to offer him one of his ravioli. At this point Maccabeo discovers the accounts book: he looks at it for a moment, then acts as if it isn't there and covers it with his plate.

'They were talking about us, but in words that stripped us of our repose,' Libera Forti cuts in, shivering slightly as if caught in a draught, and wrapping herself up in her woollen shawl. 'These memories of theirs grant us no respite, they wear us out. But look what I'm doing with the phial that I have in front of me,' and, arranging her thumb and index finger into a kind of circle, she brings her hand towards the glass and then gives it a flick with her finger: the little bottle skids away like a marble, shattering in flight. I feel very bad, I wouldn't have expected that from Libera. It means that next year I will give her a chrysanthemum.

'Well done, Libera!' little Lucia Parisi exclaims, after chewing for ages on the same mouthful as if afraid of staining the dress of which she is so fond. 'What is the point of remembering if we are not even consulted?'

'They do not consult us because they have locked us away in eternal, limitless rest,' Consiglio Parisi replies, and I can't help but notice the suggestion of a father finally speaking to his daughter, emerging for a moment from the defensive layers in which he is enveloped, 'and yet they conjure us at their pleasure. A strange error: they understand our rest on their own terms.'

'Ah, if only they found peace from their torments as they keep wandering from grave to grave. They come and weep over our heads and leave us in the damp of their tears. It's their business, obviously, and not ours. Do you want one of my ravioli?' Maccabeo lifts his plate again, and once more he ignores the accounts book underneath it.

'You eat them, old pal,' Giacinto replies courteously, chewing on a piece of bread that he has taken out of his pocket; the others don't reply.

From some corner of the house, a noise is heard. Despite the din of the rain that has begun to hammer on the roof – first in little bursts, now in a great downpour – I can hear the beginnings of a landslide.

'You heard that!' Marcello exclaims . 'You heard that!'

'Thunder, it must have been thunder,' I say hastily.

'It's a landslide.'

'Go on eating,' I say, 'it's time for the chestnut and stuffed fig fagottini. I've taken a lot of trouble this year. Just wait till you see how delicious they are.'

The groaning noise from the attic becomes clearer, draws closer, as if walking over our heads. When the roar drowns out the noise of the rain it will be time, but until then I'm not going to take an interest. I start serving dessert, showing a certain pride at the way the dish has turned out, not least aesthetically. The fagottini look like tiny pillows of puff pastry, stuffed with a cream made with chestnut flour mixed with bitter chocolate. I cook them in boiling oil, which gives them their light texture. I sometimes add cinnamon to the mixture and, to the outer crust, a cloud of icing sugar. But the best bit is the stuffed figs, a triumph of delicacy. The Alento fig tree was famed for its sweet fruits with their white pulp, ideal for drying. Now, in some overgrown gardens, I still find figs, which I dry in their skins, and when it's time, particularly at Christmas, I stuff them with walnuts or almonds, aniseed and lemon zest; then they're baked in the oven. Before bringing them to the table I cover them in melted chocolate, which quickly solidifies so they look like little black polished boxes, intensely sweet. My guests love them and scoff them down to the last one, after which they take sips of water so as not to lose the taste in their mouths.

I look at them, I can't help looking at my guests, so much at ease in death, talking calmly and seriously and raising their glasses. After the end, I think, they will take us to a place like this, surrounded with people, a gleaming banquet in the desert. Placed on the table, laid for a feast, will be the prospect of a name long since faded among the gravestones, and all effort will melt away.

'My friends,' – after probing his teeth with a wooden toothpick that he took from his pocket, Consiglio Parisi begins to speak, turning at last to Marcello and me, 'we know how surprised you are to see us so different from our reputation, so much so that you go on conjuring up the past time after time to remind us who we are. Let me tell you this: you are mistaken if you imagine that we long for the things of which we speak, or that, on the contrary, we are offended by them,' and meanwhile he picks up the lamp next to his place card, looks at it, then sets it down and covers it with his napkin.

'Quite honestly, we ourselves do not weep, as the poet has it, beneath the groaning, smoky cypress tree, we do not huddle close together as we once did by the fireside,' Giacinto interrupts, and as he speaks I see a filament of fig stuck between his teeth, but say nothing. 'In fact,' he goes on, 'what do we mean by smoky? And besides, why should we stick to the miserable habit of weeping, even once we are under the earth? Suffering is not in itself a crown of glory, by heavens! And who ever had a fire to hug beside? The mountain wind that rapped like a beggar on the door was, more than anything else, a companion in those solitary evenings. Had we been alive at the time we might weep now. But the story you tell is a different one.' At that moment Giacinto rises slightly from his chair, takes out his braided cap, sets it on his head for a moment and studies his reflection in the silver blade of the knife; then takes it off, grips it in his hands for a moment and flings it from him, so that it lands on Gideon's collar. The old dog, now stiff with arthritis, grumbles a little at the impact but calms down as soon as Giacinto raises his hands in apology.

I find myself wondering what story we are telling. A story of exclusion, without a doubt, but also of dissipated lives, lived without cries or gestures. The story of a broody hen that sleeps in the straw for years and wakes to find its brood all dead. They are speaking as if telling a tale of penitence, although one not followed by repentance.

'We are a crowd of the invisible, banished swiftly from your lives,' says Cola Forti, interrupting my confused thoughts, 'a crowd that remains in the obscurity of the village. You were quick to free yourselves of us. It was right, too, the past belongs to the dead, we can agree on that. You were the eternal present and we the ballast, the imposture to be confined where a disbelieving voice recited the prayer for the dead. You were sure that you couldn't do without us. Reasonable enough, if you'll forgive me. But now that your houses too are about to consign themselves to the soil, now you call for time to go backwards, that we may feel the weight of the earth on our shoulders.'

'You summon us to the light from a lost world,' Consiglio Parisi cuts in, his darting eyes blackening, 'you are demanding an explanation of individual lives, when they were part of a place and a community. We can no longer bear the weight of all this, just to ease a weight of yours. Besides, the butterfly that shakes the dust from its wings before resuming its flight cares little for the remains of the chrysalis in which it once lived. Why do you seem to be unaware of that?'

'I am not,' I reply, with a hint of unpleasantness in my voice that surprises me. 'I'm here to defend you, to say that you, poor things, were cogs in a mechanism of subjection for which you were not responsible. Marcello, tell them that I have always defended them.'

'Estella, what are you talking about?' he asks, distracted as usual.

'Please tell them how dear they are to me.'

'Tell who?'

'My guests.'

'Estella, you're starting to worry me.'

'We don't need anyone to defend us,' Consiglio Parisi resumes, 'each one of us is dealing with the mortification of a life that wasn't saved. I, for example, beat my children in the house, I abused my wife; I unleashed my rancour on them, a rage that came from without, from being beaten in my turn. I lived as a fool. I died as a fool. Is it really necessary for me to remember, over and over, only to keep you company because the weight of loneliness is destroying you?'

At that point I decide to do without the old words, kind but hesitant, and instead to use new, frank ones, escaping the shackle of recounted words in which I had bound myself until then, just to earn their respect.

'Where is the shame?' I ask Consiglio Parisi. 'Tell me where the shame is in trying to sweeten our own loneliness.'

'There is no shame,' he replies. 'If only, to keep from seeing your own reflection in us, you did not force us to remember the breaths, the worries, the thousand exhaustions of our past lives. You stir up our memories, drawing memories out of the dead land. You do it to impose guilt upon us, so that there is none left for you: that way your failure will be ours, and you will emerge unblemished.'

'So that's how it is,' I say quickly, because the discussion is taking an unexpected turn. 'Just outside, the past is dying before anything has been born. I knocked at your doors to escape the present, but perhaps there are doors that open to the void? If that's how it is, all efforts fall short. The house, heavy and ungainly now, is about to drag with it, brick by brick, the memory of my days. You will not return and then loneliness will be like a putrescence in my ageing flesh, a vice to which I am condemned.'

'There are no doors opening to the void, since we exist,' Cola Forti replies. 'But if, as is obvious, you have such need of us, you should at least avoid putting us on constant trial from which there is no escape. Sentence us once and for all, as they did with Pope Formosus, but free us of the weight of what we never were.'

It seems hardly coincidental that Cola Forti should have remembered Formosus, who we were told about in the convent. They put his cadaver on trial. In his empty sockets they read his soul, they caught answers from his dead mouth. Once sentence was passed they undressed him (and he appeared naked, his flesh tormented by his hairshirt, which went untouched), they amputated three of his fingers and threw them in the river, from which they floated to the surface. The order was given for all images of him to be erased, wherever they might be. His face was chiselled even from the frescoes. The trial of the corpse was celebrated to destroy the shadow, to sever once and for all the bond that connected the dead pope to the memory that the living had of him.

'You had good shoes, the roads stretched out in front of you, and you didn't know how to walk,' Consiglio Parisi begins, even more ferociously, abruptly inserting himself into my reflections. 'At this point you should have the courage to tell us how you have changed the laws of the world, with regard to the world that we have found. Perhaps such fools as I was don't go on living as fools and dying in the same way? In the end you deliver the sentence, but free us of our not having been, if you want us to free you from the guilt of not having done better, of the indignity of existing as if you were the dead and we the living.'

'What my father is trying to say,' little Lucia chimes in, and I'm surprised that she mentions her blood tie with Parisi, so I squint quizzically in such a way that she repeats what she has said, 'what my father is trying to say is that your judgement is combined with the severe judgement that we already have of ourselves, but you don't consider that our assessment of you might be equally harsh,' and, with the last of her resistance broken down, she begins to unwrap her present, after checking its consistency with her fingers. Once the tinfoil is open, she sees the chocolate at last: she smiles, little Lucia smiles, and it is obvious that she would like to eat it. Then she looks at her father as if seeking his approval, but Consiglio goes on darting his eyes about and ignores her. A moment later Lucia bites off a good-sized piece of chocolate and chews it with satisfaction.

I want to tell Marcello what has just happened in front of my eyes. While the others froze, the little one took and enjoyed her present. I make no secret of the fact that this partially reconciles me to the evening, but there would be no point explaining that to Marcello. Now there is this evening, and I am in its thrall. This is where I find myself, this is where I wish to be.

'Estella, my dear,' Libera says, turning to me and rousing me from my peaceful contemplation, 'tell me, if you can, what has changed since the days when my tooth was broken on the bar of the nuptial bed. Then as now, women are as fields exposed to the wind, with all the signs of devastation; they live with the flesh, and in the things of the flesh they die.' As she speaks she takes the woollen shawl from her shoulders and drapes it around mine. 'Take it, you'll be cold out there,' she says to me. Then, waving a finger like a wand, she turns to Marcello and says, 'And what have you done with your privilege that you are here on your own this evening, amidst all this death?'

Marcello doesn't reply.

'Hey, Marcello!' I join in. 'Libera asked you a question.'

'Libera who?' he replies, as if suddenly dragged from a state of torpor.

'Libera Forti. Aren't you listening? She asked you what you're doing here, this evening?'

'Good question. What I'm doing here? I'm doing exactly what any desperate man would do who loves and cannot know if his love will ever be returned: his head rolling backwards to be picked up again later; his arms braced for the next round of torment; dull-witted surrender to illusions. Illusions, that's exactly it. They're like sheep: they help with the sleep of the meek, and the empty bellies of the poor; creatures who live and die like fools.

'That's it!' Maccabeo interjects. 'I'm sorry to say so, but as Marcello demonstrates with his sorrowful words, we're always invisible to someone.'

At this point I bring my hands together as old women do in church as a sign of excessive faith, but in fact I'm doing it to distract Marcello from replying to Maccabeo's words. In fact he doesn't reply, as if he hasn't heard them.

'Don't worry, my friends, about the objections that will be made to you,' says Cola Forti, who must have noticed my bewilderment. 'Look around you: what do you see? We see empty clothes. Look at your lives, look at them closely: why are you troubled? Do you have an idea that you believe in? It seems to me that there is nothing left: no opinions, no aspirations, nothing whatsoever. And yet with unfathomable arrogance you rub raw the rosary of your accusations, without bearing in mind that what you are in fact doing is filling your void with past lives. You, so tenaciously alive, have deaths to deal with and you won't let them go.' At this point Cola Forti picks up the jute pouch that he had thrown under the table, after taking it out of the glass, checks that no buttons have fallen on the ground and puts it in his pocket.

I think I can consider myself satisfied: two of my guests have appreciated the little tribute I have dreamt up for them. This evening was my greatest desire. Obviously Marcello pretends not to have seen it; he doesn't even turn towards us.

'For my part, just call for me,' says little Lucia, who always says little, out of her ancient habit of silence which she has never shed. 'I will never say no to a delicious meal, particularly if chocolate is involved,' she goes on, 'but please free me from the weight of a life that I brought pointlessly to an end, if the memory of those days still weighs so heavily upon my poor bones.'

'Wretched is he who is beneath the earth as he was above it,' Consiglio Parisi cuts in; he is finally calm, his eyes have stopped wandering and they no longer seem pitch-black.

'If you can't do without us,' he goes on, 'just summon us, but not to remind us who we are. Summon us to clad us in airy attire. Relieve us of our dusty suffering, don't be so mean as to leave us with scraps. Let us walk among you on puppet steps, light and mercurial. Summon us that we may change our destinies.'

'Change your destinies. What does that mean?' I ask, narrowing my eyes, but in fact I am thinking of the earth that covers them and which will by now have learned their names.

'It means removing us from the world and its concerns, removing us from this biting cold. I, for example, would happily return, but not to be as before. Bring me back to my house, down in the countryside, among my children, but make me a loving father more blessed with good fortune. Put in my hands a gift for my wife, an elegant dress or a flower; make us dance in our sitting room, uncomfortable though it was.'

In the fire's dying flames, words rise gently. The candles have melted to different degrees of liquefaction, even though they were lit at the same moment: some flames are going out, others are still high. The white spirit in the little lamp has almost run out. I pretend to be fascinated by the inlay of the tablecloth, then I consider my hands, putting one on the other, several times, then I stretch my fingers, one two three *uh!* there are ten of them, now they're in a ball; what I really want to do is keep my eyes lowered and say nothing, but I also know that they will interpret the movements of my face, the veins on my neck, pulsing madly.

'They say it all ends with death,' old Maccabeo says in a conciliatory tone, 'but in the end what do those who assert such a thing really know about it? Ultimately it is merely their opinion. What I want to say to you, now that dinner is over, is that from where we are we can tell you much more about yourselves than you seem to know about us. If death has come, my dear friends, it too has passed. That is why we exist, and the void does not. The *Here lies...*

that you write upon our graves does not always mean here, in the earth, where the crows bleakly gather. You can see us more cheerfully in the evening, when the stars come out. Look for us in a grey stone in the sun, in the song of a bird freed from pain.'

Overcome by their words, stunned and perhaps also slightly offended, I get up and go and open the shutters. I am bad, I know, but for a moment I would like them to see themselves, to tremble at the sight. I have been chilled by the evidence that they have produced. They have delivered judgement upon us, ruthless judgement. The house brusquely reproaches me: a tiny pebble falls among the knots of the macramé, followed by a stream of white dust.

'Are you sure this isn't a landslide?' Marcello says.

I nod and close the shutters immediately.

At that precise moment, as happens every time, they should get to their feet, and indeed they get to their feet; they should prepare to leave, and they prepare to do so; the dog should bark, and indeed it barks. They bid us a hasty farewell with the words 'Another time, friends', and the only smile is for old Gideon, who walks them whining to the door and immediately begins to wait again.

'The moment when they go away is painful, in spite of the unease into which they throw me every time,' I say to Marcello, who is brushing from his jacket the plaster dust that has fallen on him.

'You should look into the condition of the house. Can't you see what's happening?'

'I am not leaving this house.'

'But it won't survive the rain of another winter.'

'I'm not leaving.'

'Look at me, I'm covered with bits of plaster that are falling everywhere. I don't want to die under a beam.'

'Then go. I know that we are never ready to die, which is why I will die alone,' and as I see it I turn my eyes towards the sky, in the pose of one who is about to be martyred.

'Do your jokes, then, it's all you ever do. I'm off. See you tomorrow?' he says in a single breath, inadvertently striking a very intimate note.

'Who knows,' and I barely conceal a smile. Then, when he's about to leave the room, I call him back: 'Marcello,' I say, lingering on the 'l's because I've always liked the sound his name makes, 'on the counter by the kitchen sink you'll find the ceramic bowl, the one with the verdigris ferns: it's full of zabaglione.'

The house breathes heavily, it's like a dying animal; it struggles to hold its beams steady, it squeezes its walls together, arms gripping a belly. It struggles to breathe out once, twice. The water seeping from the attic has the consistency of sweat, icy sweat that runs along the walls, still decorated for a party; it soaks the geometric ceiling frieze, it flows through the paintwork, which surrenders its pigment.

Outside, the wind is no longer a breath unheard, it's a raging fury that beats against the panes. The window holds for a minute, then yields and flies open: the exhausted glass is on the floor, the iron frame too.

The rain is ceaseless, it hammers like footsteps above my head, every now and again accompanied by a light, a brief illusion, and the darkness immediately returns. In those few moments of illuminated night I see the elm tree still standing, untroubled by the vision of decline.

The attic swells worryingly, but I walk beneath it anyway, nothing can happen to me in here. I move from one room to the next, picking up little things that might be useful to me during the night, which I will spend under the tree. I start up the stairs and keep stumbling. I struggle to my room, where the plaster dust has already coated the floor. I take two or three books, a candle and an old tin box containing an amber pendant that I slipped from my mother's neck on the night of my departure. I hurry back down. The sound of glasses shattering as they fall from the dresser simulates a flicker of the heart before sleep. The pointless harvest of old splendour is about to rot beneath the rain that is now starting, the ever-fainter clip-clop sound, with the last droplets of water making sad wreaths of flowers. The house is on the edge now, a scrappy feather

that could be toppled with a breath. And yet it resists,
out of stubbornness, or pride, or who knows what mystery.
The immemorial silence returns: my last dwelling place
flung far by the night; the house that lies with the world
around it has survived, safe once more, at least for now.

There is movement beneath the elm tree. The square,
deserted until a moment before, is now filled with people.
I step forward. On the bench – which should also have been
removed in its day – is Lucia Parisi, sewing a dress with
gold rings on it. She inserts the needle and brings it up into
the air, imagining herself in some fairy-tale or other, as I
can tell by the smile that occupies half of her face; not the
other half, the other half is serious, perhaps because it falls
beneath the serious eye of her father, who stands to her left.

Next to Consiglio Parisi is a little white coffin secured
by a network of ropes to pull it. Now he sits down on the
bench, almost turning his back to Lucia, who doesn't seem
to notice; then he grabs a branch of the elm tree, pulls on
it as if to break it, then lets it go; at last he leans over the
coffin, pushes the ropes aside and removes the lid: the
corpse, little Mariuccia, rests on the wooden bed. A startled
fly falls upon the girl's face, but Consiglio waves it away.

The moment is spoiled by old Maccabeo striding
impetuously into the square. As soon as he is under the elm
tree, he takes a handkerchief from a pocket and wipes his
forehead, as if after making a great effort.

'My dear Parisi, I need your help,' he says, approaching
him and taking him by an arm as if to take him away.

'Steady, Maccabeo. Don't you see what I have to do?'

'I just see you lazing about.'

'I have to keep the flies off Mariuccia.'

'There you have it, old man, it was flies I wanted to talk to you about: I've had a brilliant idea, a lifetime's work.'

'What are you talking about?'

'My sons are about to come back from the front and I have to reopen the shop for this evening, but I need you to give me a hand lifting the shutter, because the hinges are jammed with rust.'

'And what do flies have to do with it?'

'This is the good bit! My plan is to breed all kinds of flies, particularly blowflies and flesh flies, and sell them, still pupating, to my clientele. Don't you think that's an exciting idea? And besides, let's admit it, flies deserve much more than we usually give them. I am sorry to say so, but these creatures are unfairly maligned as ugly and harmful, when in fact they are very useful.'

'I don't follow, Maccabeo, and I'm really not very interested in this,' Parisi replies in a harsh voice.

'Listen to what I'm saying. How many times have you said disparaging things about these little beasts? "They're dropping like flies", or "No flies on him". And to cap it all, "He wouldn't hurt a fly". Not to mention "Seven flies with one blow". As if flies had no right not to be swatted or killed, as if they couldn't feel grand in their smallness, calm in their journeys through the air; as if they couldn't die of loneliness, or as if they deserved no better death than the sweet lie of flypaper. For all these reasons I intend to breed them and draw profit from it, now that my sons are about to resume the reins of our trade. Don't you think it's a brilliant idea? More than anything else, I predict that fly-breeding will be the business of the future.'

'To be quite honest I think it's a ludicrous idea, but I have no time to argue,' and with a swift wave of the hand

Consiglio dismisses Maccabeo, before wiping away with the sleeve of his jacket some saliva that has trickled from Mariuccia's mouth.

Maccabeo looks thoughtfully around, studies the groups of people who have gathered in the square and runs towards the biggest of them.

'You know my friends, Antonio and Luchino are about to return from the front. I have to reopen the shop. It all has to be ready for this evening,' he exultantly informs each man and woman who catches his eye. Some stop to listen, others walk on. There is a hubbub in the square, here a seller of wildflowers, there a little kiosk selling fresh lemonade. Under the stone gate marking the entrance to the square there are two chairs supporting a box of vegetables. A woman with a kerchief around her head shouts: 'Fresh greens! Medical herbs!' Stepping forward, I recognise her. She's a Paudice, from the family that miraculously survived the collapse of the house.

It is at that moment that Consiglio, ignoring the racket around him, rises to his feet and walks towards the edge of the village, to the beginning of the dirt road that leads to Terzo di Mezzo. As he walks homewards, he pulls behind him the little white coffin, which bounces slightly on the cobbles polished by the friction of time.

I pass the square and begin to walk along the little road leading to the *trazzera degli stranieri*, the path to the mountain. From that point onwards the way is uphill, and in two hours' walk you reach the top, which from there is a strip of rock surrounded by a jumble of trees.

Along the twisting path up to the peak stands the Forti house. Under the pergola, filled again with vine leaves, Libera and Cola are playing with buttons. I recognise the game of *staccia*, in which each player throws his buttons into a square of earth and then, with a flat stone, tries to push them towards an imaginary goal. The Fortis are almost coming to blows because they've put money on the game. I step forward to listen.

'That men are all equal in the end is a great idea, an idea worth betting on,' Cola cries, throwing the stone that sends his button towards the goal.

'You're talking about men, as always. I bet on women, on their reign which will come one day,' and Libera too throws the stone that pushes her button towards its goal.

The point of the game is for one of the buttons to reach the goal first, but in throwing the stones with unusual force they have shattered them both. The game has to be replayed, with different and less fragile buttons.

That's what they do, I think. They bring us to a certain point and then they leave, because they prefer to set up house among the brambles, among the trembling trees, in the running water, while they are thought to be closed away in the earthly confines of a grave.

Here, among these stones that have been commandeered by nature in the strangest ways, it isn't like walking in places where there is nothing, because they are there. From this perspective, happier at least than the tomb, they can sew patches on the coarse jackets of those who have lived unhappy lives – silence in silence – now that death can no longer come, now that even the end, if it came, has gone. It is in fact possible to try, I'm only saying try, to change destinies, as after a convalescence; to reverse the course of lives thrust into the cold and give them back a little warmth as if it were a new life, now that the other, infuriating one has reached its conclusion. 'Summon us to clad us in airy garments,' Consiglio Parisi said a short while ago. 'Summon us to change our destinies.'

I move away, and wherever I look the walls of the houses are lit by the radiant beam of the lamps. A woman beats a carpet on the edge of the balcony, and as she does so she scatters pebbles that rain down on an old man sitting on a little chair, leaning against the wall of the floor below; the old man looks at the woman in bafflement but doesn't move and, turning his eyes to the sky, says, 'Make sure it holds, make sure it holds,' referring to the balcony. I too am struck by a bit of dust, soiling my velvet dress, but I can't worry about that now. The old residents have returned, they have returned at last. Among them are those who left for distant lands and never came back. I see their weary faces, drawn after the long journey, and yet stunned, struck by the wonder of return. I walk back towards the square and along the way I draw up with good old Giacinto, his braided cap squashed on his head and a wooden wine-funnel for making his announcements. He seems worried, and I notice a quiver in his eyes, like a nervous tic.

'What's the rush, Giacinto? Important news to deliver?'

'By Jerusalem, what news! The old inhabitants have come back.'

'So what's the point of announcing it? They all know that already.'

'Things haven't happened until they're said. That's why I'm going to say it.' He walks away with a firm and measured tread, leaving me behind.

The silence to which I had grown accustomed in the years of abandonment seems remote. A long silence, occasionally interrupted by crashes from the houses that once held so much time and so much human labour. Even the darkness, total before, is broken now by chinks of light peeping from the houses and the little workshops.

I am distracted by a smell coming up from the street, the smell of earth and fire burning among the stones. In a corner between two houses, a band of children are roasting chestnuts, pulling them from the fire with the tip of a twig.

I notice that the flowers I dropped in the graves as tributes to the dead whose memory I preserve have disappeared. The children are jumping into them and their cries are a source of comfort, like the velvety murmur emerging from the houses.

I notice a dog staring at me with meek, almost blind eyes. Then, as dogs sometimes do, it starts yelping and flattens itself against the ground. I walk over and recognise Gideon, now joined by a pack of dogs emerging from an alleyway, sheepdogs, long and thin. They bark lazily, but don't keep me from stroking my friend, who gets to his feet and joins me, ready to resume my walk towards the square.

I feel as if I have returned to that far-off day when I came back here with Gideon by my side, beneath the lashing snow, before the village that didn't recognise me and the church that offered us shelter from the cold. Tonight I want to go into the church, having stopped circling God, having survived a pain that would bend mountains. Gideon walks a little way ahead of me, stopping and waiting for me every now and again, seeming to say, 'Look up at the passing stars. Look at this night, brighter than the day.' When we have almost reached the square in front of the church I become aware of someone following me, but I don't slow down. I turn swiftly around: an old woman dressed in black, with a conical wicker basket on her back, studies me and a moment later opens her mouth in amazement.

Then she says, 'Do you recognise me?'

'No,' I say.

'Why not? One day I lent you some clothes, you were where you are at this moment, quite naked.'

'I remember now. What's your name?'

'Mariuccia,' she replies, and I observe her face, a multitude of wrinkles crossed by something like a smile.

'My dear Mariuccia, you left in such a hurry that day that I didn't have the chance to thank you. Is there something I can do for you in return?'

'There is one thing, in fact. Do you know how to read?'

'Yes, Mariuccia.'

'Could you read a letter for me? It's from Michelino, my son who left for Venezuela. I don't know how to read.'

'Do you have it with you?'

'I always keep it with me,' and as if she expected nothing else, the old woman takes the basket off her back, sets it on the ground and takes out a folded cloth, from which with two fingers she pulls the letter kept inside and hands it to me.

In a few lines, her son tells her that he is based in Caracas but doesn't intend to stay there for long, since he misses his mother and the village. As soon as he can, he will set off on the return journey, even if it is expensive, even though there is so much sea in between. He will write to her soon, even though she doesn't know how to read; the words of a son who has never forgotten his mother's efforts to give him shoes and good clothes are bound to reach her, he is sure. He loves her with tender affection.

'What does he say?' the old woman asks me.

'He says that he is well, that he is based in Caracas and that he will leave soon to come back here,' I reply.

'And me, does he ask about me?'

'He hopes that you are enjoying good health, he says he thinks of you always and can't wait to hug you again.'

'It's not true. Why are you telling me lies?'

'Lies?'

'That's not what the letter says.'

'It does, I'm telling you.'

'No, signora. In the letter it says that Michelino despises me.'

'Mariuccia, I don't know what makes you say that, especially given that you can't read, but I assure you that on this sheet of paper it says that Michelino loves you with very tender affection and thanks you for the sacrifices you have made for him.

'Michelino never came back and my heart dried up.'

'He'll come back, you'll see, like the others.'

The old woman takes the letter from my hands and puts it back in the cloth. Then, putting her load on her back again, she smiles and says goodbye. She walks away slowly, a black figure that can't be more than four foot six inches tall. Before she disappears, swallowed up by the road, she turns round for a moment, raises her hand and waves.

A cloud slips across the disc of the moon and for a moment everything is dark. Soon the cloud moves into the night, and in the moonlight Giacinto reappears, the funnel to his mouth.

Note on the Text

Alento is an abandoned village that lives in my imagination,
like the characters who unwittingly populate it. When
I started writing this novel, I wanted to tell the story
of Roscigno Vecchia and its last inhabitant – and to some
degree I went to specific sources, a specific geography
– but then I decided that Alento should represent not only
a particular abandoned town, and that it should include
more than a story of loneliness. For me, the houses rotting
in silence are a temporary dwelling, a place to be, if only
for a while. I was born in one of those surviving places
where past and present touch, and in fact you only have to
cross a street to find yourself face to face with a dilapidated
house. I myself have lived in a big house that was collapsing
around me, in those shapeless years when you have every
possibility in front of you, or none. Immersed as I was
in silence, I often crossed the threshold of an abandoned
house and imagined the people who had lived there coming
back. I almost always changed their destinies.

As I wrote, I recovered fragments of memory from the
cracks in the walls, the nooks and hiding places of those
torn houses. However, I had to rename things to make them
exist, and to exist more deeply. I sought words to express
not so much a reflection on the ruins but a way of inhabiting
them, discovering their clandestine life. From the ruins I
drew a reversed perspective, like an invitation to resistance:
I saw a possibility in things left to wander, in uselessness.
So, taking care of all this pure, dense nothingness became
a way of being in the world, among so many possible worlds.
I was helped by poetry, that poor and precious thing, that
thing which, of all things, is an experience of the world, an

act of peace. I was helped by poets, starting with Alfonso Gatto, with whom I also have certain family connections. But there are many poets from whom I draw experience and sometimes comfort. As a kind of repayment I will name them all, the ones that are known and, more importantly, the ones who are forgotten. I name those who have in some way something to do with the drafting of this novel: Leopardi and Caproni; Pascoli, Montale and Mark Strand; Vittorio Sereni and Rilke, who also provided the title, from his 'Autumn' in the *Book of Images*; Borges, Charles Wright, Cortázar, Emily Dickinson, Mariangela Gualtieri, Pier Luigi Cappello, Yves Bonnefoy, Marina Tsvetaeva, Birago Diop, Antonia Pozzi, Beppe Salvia, Nadia Campana, all the way to the very forgotten Nedda Falzolgher. The almost literal quotations come from 'Convito d'ombre' by Pascoli, 'Requiem for a Friend' and the tenth Duino Elegy by Rilke; from 'Adam Cast Forth' and 'The Night They Kept Vigil in the South' by Borges, and his 'Fragments of an Apocryphal Gospel'.

One crucial piece of reading was *Il giorno del giudizio* by Salvatore Satta, to which I tried to pay tribute in the stories; equally important were the tales of Silvio D'Arzo, the writings of Charles Dickens and of Elsa Morante, Guglielmo Petroni, Gogol, Fuks, Tommaso Landolfi, Guido Piovene, Nuto Revelli (in particular *L'anello forte. La donna: storie di vita contadina*), and of course Moravia.

The novel contains certain historical documents, adapted for the purposes of the narrative. These are the cards from the front in the story of Maccabeo. For these I accessed the archive of the Fondazione/laboratorio di Capaccio Paestum; in particular the publication *Un soldato di Capaccio nella Prima Guerra Mondiale. Cartoline dal fronte*

1916–1918 (ed. Maria Teresa Schiavino and Sergio Vecchio, Arci Postiglione, 2003). The Quaderni Arci Postiglione were indispensable for the diaries of the time presented in adapted form in the story of Cola Forti. The local history writings of Domenico Romagnano, especially those contained in the collection *Il volto della mia terra* (Bemporad Marzocco, 1960), led me in the definition of the character of Giacinto, whose story contains references to characters that existed in real life, while the events involving them and the narrated episodes are entirely invented. For the story of Roscigno Vecchia I consulted the essay *Storia di Roscigno e dei suoi trasferimenti* by Maria Laura Castellano (Giannini Editore, 2008). I was able to read the story of Formoso in the book *Papa Formoso, processo al cadaver* by Mario Bacchiega (Bastogi Editrice Italiana, 1983). For some of Marcello's reflections on *bifolchi* (yokels) I consulted *The Moral Basis of a Backward Society* by Edward C. Banfield (Free Press, 1958). I also read *Animismo o Spiritismo?* by Ernesto Bozzano (Editrice Luce e Ombra, 1967) and Allan Kardec's *Revue Spirite 1858–1869*.

The biographies of the characters are imaginary. So are the places around Alento, the streets, the arrangement of the mountains and the caves, which exist in this way only in my fantasy. What does exist as I have described it, however, is the area of Terzo di Mezzo where, completely run down and full of cracks and ivy, the house of those formless years still lives.

Acknowledgements

I am grateful to my Facebook friends: it was their posts that gave birth to the nucleus of this book; to Massimo Onofri for lingering a little longer on those posts, the first pieces of writing; to Alessandro Bertante and Davide Morganti, for the same reason; to Andrea Di Consoli, friend and brother, who gave a recognisable form to my cure for abandonment.

I thank Sergio Vecchio for putting at my disposal the post-cards from his private archive, and Oreste Mottola.

I thank Patrizia Rinaldi, not least for the help that she gave me at certain points with Cecco. And to Vicki Satlow who is here, always firm with me as well as reassuring.

Thanks to my female friends and the words that I couldn't do without: Emanuela Ersilia Abbadessa, Laura Bettanin, Sara Gamberini, Isabella Mattazzi, Francesca Serafini, Anna Stefi. To Anna I also owe the title of the novel and a certain way of being; to Sara the sounds of odd-number days.

Thanks to Vincenzo Pardini, always there, as a discreet father. Likewise to Giovanni De Luna, Francesco De Core, Antonio Di Grado, Elvira Seminara, Nicoletta Pellegrino, Ilario Massarelli, Carlo Ziviello.

I would like to thank Andrea Caterini, Barbara Garlaschelli, Francesca Magni, Margherita Oggero, Luciana Petroni, for reading the drafts of this novel. Special thanks to Simone Caltabellota, Andrea De Benedeti and Silverio Novelli.

Thanks to Chiara Belliti who, between an amen and various soufflés, listened to the voices of the dead. Thanks to Andrea who gave me a place to live, between things visible and invisible. Thanks to Lucia Pellegrino, who told me silenced or buried stories.

Forthcoming

(type 2 – prose)
Prairie, Dresses, Art, Other by Danielle Dutton (2024)
The Seers by Sulaiman Addonia (2024)

Back Catalogue

(type 1 – poetry)
Plainspeak by Astrid Alben (2019)
Safe Metamorphosis by Otis Mensah (2020)
Republic Of Dogs/Republic Of Birds by Stephen Watts (2016/2020)
Home by Emily Critchley (2021)
Away From Me by Caleb Klaces (2021)
Path Through Wood by Sam Buchan-Watts (2021)
Two Twin Pipes Sprout Water by Lila Matsumoto (2021)
Deltas by Leonie Rushforth (2022)
Island mountain glacier by Anne Vegter, trans. Astrid Alben (2022)
Little Dead Rabbit by Astrid Alben (2022)
Emblem by Lucy Mercer (2022)
Twenty-Four Hours by Stephen Watts (2022)
A History by Dan Burt (2022)
Journeys Across Breath: Poems 1975–2005 by Stephen Watts (2022)
Artifice by Lavinia Singer (2023)
Incubation: a space for monsters by Bhanu Kapil (2023)
Monochords by Yannis Ritsos, trans. Paul Merchant, with Chiara Ambrosio (2023)
Virgula by Sasja Janssen, trans. Michele Hutchison (2024)

(type 2 – prose)
Fatherhood by Caleb Klaces (2019)
I'm Afraid That's All We've Got Time For by Jen Calleja (2020)
The Boiled in Between by Helen Marten (2020)
Along the River Run by Paul Buck (2020)
Lorem Ipsum by Oli Hazzard (2021)
The Weak Spot by Lucie Elven (2021)
Deceit by Yuri Felsen, trans. Bryan Karetnyk (2022)
Our Last Year by Alan Rossi (2022)
Vehicle: a verse novel by Jen Calleja (2023)

Lori & Joe by Amy Arnold (2023)
Pleasure Beach by Helen Palmer (2023)

(type 3 – interdisciplinary projects)
alphabet poem: for kids! by Emily Critchley, Michael Kindellan
& Alison Honey Woods (2020)
The sea is spread and cleaved and furled by Ahren Warner (2020)
Songs for Ireland by Robert Herbert McClean (2020)
microbursts by Elizabeth Reeder & Amanda Thomson (2021)
Sorcerer by Ed Atkins & Steven Zultanski (2023)

(type 4 – anthologies)
Try To Be Better ed. Sam Buchan-Watts & Lavinia Singer (2019)
PROTOTYPE 1 (2019)
PROTOTYPE 2 (2020)
Intertitles: An anthology at the intersection of writing & visual art, ed.
Jess Chandler, Aimee Selby, Hana Noorali & Lynton Talbot (2021)
PROTOTYPE 3 (2021)
PROTOTYPE 4 (2022)
Strangers Within: Documentary as Encounter, ed. Therese Hennigsen
& Juliette Joffé (2022)
PROTOTYPE 5 (2023)
Seven Rooms, ed. Dominic J. Jaeckle & Jess Chandler (2023)

(House Sparrow Press)
A Sparrow's Journey: John Berger reads Andrey Platonov (2016)
Infinite Gradation by Anne Michaels (2017)
Doorways: Women, Homelessness, Trauma and Resistance, ed. Bekki
Perriman (2019)
Dialogue with a Somnambulist: Stories, Essays & a Portrait Gallery
by Chloe Aridjis (2021)
Through the Billboard Promised Land Without Ever Stopping by Derek
Jarman (2022)

( ) (   ) p   prototype

poetry / prose / interdisciplinary projects / anthologies

Creating new possibilities in the publishing of fiction and poetry
through a flexible, interdisciplinary approach and the production
of unique and beautiful books.

Prototype is an independent publisher working across genres
and disciplines, committed to discovering and sharing work that
exists outside the mainstream.

Each publication is unique in its form and presentation, and
the aesthetic of each object is considered critical to its production.

Prototype strives to increase audiences for experimental
writing, as the home for writers and artists whose work requires
a creative vision not offered by mainstream literary publishers.

In its current, evolving form, Prototype consists of 4 strands
of publications:

(type 1 – poetry)
(type 2 – prose)
(type 3 – interdisciplinary projects)
(type 4 – anthologies) including an annual anthology
of new work, *PROTOTYPE*.

The Earth is Falling by Carmen Pellegrino
Published by Prototype in 2024

Copyright © Carmen Pellegrino 2015
First published as *Cade la Terra* in Italy by Giunti Editore in 2015
Translation copyright © Shaun Whiteside 2024

This book has been translated thanks to a translation
grant awarded by the Italian Ministry of Foreign Affairs
and International Cooperation.

Questo libro è stato tradotto grazie a un contributo alla
traduzione assegnato dal Ministero degli Affari Esteri e della
Cooperazione Internazionale italiano.

This book has been selected to receive financial assistance
from English PEN's PEN Translates programme, supported by
Arts Council England. English PEN exists to promote literature
and our understanding of it, to uphold writers' freedoms around
the world, to campaign against the persecution and imprisonment
of writers for stating their views, and to promote the friendly
co-operation of writers and the free exchange of ideas.
www.englishpen.org

This book has also received support from the Fondation
Jan Michalski, and from Arts Council England.

Fondation
Jan Michalski

Design by Matthew Stuart & Andrew Walsh-Lister
(Traven T. Croves)
Typeset in Marist by Seb McLauchlan
Printed in the UK by TJ Books

ISBN 978-1-913513-47-4

(type 2 – prose)
www.prototypepublishing.co.uk
@prototypepubs

prototype publishing
71 oriel road
london e9 5sg
uk